IRON
IN
THE
BLOOD

Best Wishes
Bob Oakes (alias Fred Pope)

By Frederick John Pope
Illustrated by Emma Douglas

Chapter Headings Illustrated by Barrie Dunwell

First Edition Published in 2010 by TUCANN*books*

ISBN 978-1-907516-02-3

Text © Bob Oakes 2010.
Cartoon Illustrations © Emma Douglas
Chapter Heading Illustrations by Barrie Dunwell © TUCANN*books* 2010
Design © TUCANN*books* 2010

Produced by: TUCANNdesign&print, 19 High Street, Heighington, Lincoln LN4 1RG
Tel & Fax: 01522 790009
Website. www.tucann.co.uk

I have dedicated this book to my late parents;
all four of them, without whom
I could not have forged my career.

Fascinated

Chapter 1
The spark within me

My nose was almost frozen to the murky windowpane as I peered to catch a glimpse of a swarthy figure wearing a frayed leather apron hammering away upon the anvil. I stood transfixed as showers of sparks cascaded through the air, illuminating the dimly lit room and dancing off the antiquated tools, shelves, benches and beams that were covered in a layer of a greyish brown dust, untouched by a brush for generations. I saw the forge fire brought to life by a steady pumping of a massive set of bellows, which seemed to time the rhythm and ring of the hammer upon the anvil. It was a musical accompaniment to the firework display, a bewitching sight, one that myself as an impressionable ten year old could watch for hours and incidentally, not realizing that it was setting the stage for most of my later working life.

I have often been asked if my father or any of my family had been in the trade before me and until recently had not been able to answer that question. However much later in my life, through a quirk of fate, I discovered that my great grandfather had been the blacksmith at a village in the New Forest and as trades were mostly handed down in those days, probably generations of family before him had been practicing smiths.

Having been born shortly after the Second World War and brought up in a Derbyshire colliery town by my adoptive parents, I religiously had to attend Sunday School at the local Baptist church from about the age of seven. The forge happened to be upon the one mile route to church and the blacksmith irreverently continued his trade on what my parents regarded as the Holy day, one that had to be set aside for worship and rest. Mother and Father looked forward to having me out of harm's way on a Sunday afternoon for reasons known only to themselves. Unlike this day and age, children of that time were entrusted to walk to their destination without their parents having to guard them and without fear of being harmed. I remember the three mile walk to my junior school, partly following the canal tow path, that we were entrusted to trek every day and in all weathers without adult supervision. This would be unheard of in our present day society, where four-wheel drive vehicles congest our streets, taking the little ones a few hundred yards to school. The forge became a regular staging post on the way to Sunday school and the blacksmith, whose name was Tom, would often break from his work in order to patiently answer the many questions I would fire at him; 'Why do you hit the anvil every so often and not your work?' I asked, 'Why are there so many different kinds of tongs? Have you ever burnt yourself badly? What is that which you take out from the bottom of the fire every so often and why put it on your path?'

Tom, the blacksmith, was a shy reticent character, with a long thin face, gaunt expression and short ginger hair permanently covered with an ancient flat cap, his deeply furrowed brow could have been dug by the very ploughs he repaired. Tom had a permanent stoop, probably due to many years of hammering over an anvil placed fairly low to the ground, His huge muscular arms dwarfed his rounded shoulders, he wore a leather apron over a brown waistcoat and old wool trousers with turn-ups full of hammer scale and dirt. He worked long hours, but on his way home from work Tom would call at the local alehouse to enjoy a glass of Shipstons mild ale. Initially Tom's reaction to youngsters staring through the window of the forge had been to chase us away. However, when on one occasion I plucked up courage to walk through his door and ask politely if I could watch him for a few minutes, he seemed surprised and realized that we were not hell-bent on causing mischief. Once he asked me to tidy some of cuts of iron in the corner of the forge, this made me the happiest chap alive now that I was working for my hero. Totally forgetting that I was wearing my best Sunday clothes I set to work and within ten minutes Tom had an extremely tidy corner, so out of place compared to the rest of the workshop. It was when I arrived home however, that I had some explaining to do, the dirty hands and the indelible rusty patches on my Sunday suit!

Often on my way home from day school I would walk the extra mile in order to visit Tom at his forge, hoping that he would agree to me pumping the bellows to heat up the iron that he placed among the coals of his fire. Tom was extremely reluctant to allow me to do this at first, however after much persistence on my part he agreed, but only after I promised to spend a considerable time watching carefully how they were used. The huge circular double acting bellows were an impressive sight, Tom kept the leather clean and supple with regular application of 'neats-foot oil'. The end of the long wooden handle terminated with a cow horn attached and the balance being provided by two massive spherical iron weights hanging from the movable part of the frame, ensuring they were easy to operate and without much effort. Tom explained that the art of using the bellows correctly could only be acquired over a long period of time, that it was important to obtain a smooth consistent flow of air rather than an uneven staccato of spasmodic gasps. I had to learn how to control the air

Tom's Forge

flow in order to produce fierce and gentle heats as and when required and to refrain from blowing the coals clean out of the fire. On the many future occasions that Tom allowed me to operate the bellows, I studied him working at the anvil, manipulating the hot iron with hammer and tongs. Subconsciously I learned much that stood me in good stead for the time when I would eventually be earning my living at the craft.

My adoptive parents failed to understand my fascination for the forge, and Father only allowed my visits there due to the realization that I could have been getting up to far more mischief hanging around with my school chums of which he totally disapproved. To him it happened to be the lesser of the two evils. Certainly no one within the family had any leanings towards the craft of the blacksmith.

Father worked as an inspector of spun iron pipes produced by the local ironworks, a huge industrial complex occupying an area of five square miles, comprising an ore preparation plant, coke-ovens, blast furnaces and casting sheds. The row of three huge blast-furnaces was visible from our house some two miles distant. These eighty foot high gigantic monsters each appeared as having two massive arms, holding upwards one end of a large steel pipe which descended in the direction of a tall adjacent steel cylinder. At regular intervals, large quantities of molten slag, a useful byproduct of these furnaces, were emptied from huge ladles at the slag processing works in order to be crushed when cool for road surfacing material. The tipping of this slag would light up the sky on many a dark night, illuminating the outline of these eerie monsters by means of a massive incandescent red glow resembling the last vestiges of a powerful sun which appeared, illogically, to set in the east.

The area in which I grew up is today a treasure trove of industrial archeology, road, railway, river and canal, being in close proximity to each other. Man made hills or coal tips lie adjacent to their natural geological neighbours, having in recent years been landscaped by the appropriate authorities. Derelict railway lines have become footpaths or cycle tracks, indeed the whole area is characterised by the hammer and hand of our industrial forebears, though now the present policy of urban regeneration is in danger of obliterating the industrial past.

I still have vivid memories of the day, when as a six year old, I accompanied my mother to the hospital at Nottingham where they had taken her husband following a serious accident at work. During his lunch hour, a young worker had been showing off to his mates how well he could drive a lorry around the yard. The vehicle had been loaded with heavy cast iron water pipes that unfortunately had not been secured to the trailer. On turning a corner, one of the pipes rolled off crushing my father's left leg. The injuries received necessitated the amputation of the limb below the knee. This traumatic incident obviously had a profound effect upon the whole family, who rallied round to offer physical, moral and spiritual support at our time of need. Although being so young at the time, I made my contribution to help the situation by learning to run errands for Mother to the corner shop. After a long period of convalescence and learning how to use an artificial limb, Father returned to work, though in the revised capacity of an office worker.

Although an extremely intelligent and intellectual person, Father had been made to leave school at the age of twelve, during the great depression, in order to supplement the frugal income of the poor mining family to which he belonged. Had he been allowed to continue at school, I am sure that he would have had the opportunity of a more rewarding professional career. He was fond of reading social history, particularly Victorian novels written by the Bronte Sisters and books by Charles Dickens. Later in retirement he became a keen member of the Bronte' Society, as well as being in great demand as an authoritative public speaker on the subject. I now firmly believe that any further academic or social ambition became thwarted by his passion for evangelical religious fundamentalism. The Christian faith however, supported his life especially through difficult times, such as his accident at work and I have much to be grateful for in the way by which my adoptive parents helped provide me with a very structured upbringing and education.

The accident proved to be just one more addition to a whole series of tragic events that had befallen his life since his marriage before the war. John, his five year old son, had been killed in a road traffic accident, when a lorry collided with my Uncle's milk cart on which the boy had been a passenger. Christina, his sister, had been born premature and died at two weeks old. Due to Mother suffering a nervous breakdown, Father had now been recalled, on compassionate leave, from serving as a sergeant with the British army in India and therefore having to forfeit his rank. Their Christian beliefs again supported them through their tragic moments, resulting in the positive moves for my adoption, by wishing to resolve the loss of their family and completely making a new start.

Upon reaching senior school, I was introduced to the study of metalwork, a subject hardly taught in the curriculum today. It is indeed a crying shame that so many schools have now abandoned any tuition in traditional craft subjects, I have always held to the view, that the ability to design stems from an intimate knowledge of tools materials and processes and it is unfortunate that the majority of today's pupils and students are denied the wonderful experience of practical creativity. Learning metalwork skills gave me the opportunity to practice some basic forge-work and associated techniques.

Our teacher had been a blacksmith in industry during the war and had retrained at Loughborough College in order to teach technical subjects in secondary education. He introduced me to books showing photographs of work produced by the German blacksmith Fritz Khun . Although these publications are for the time being out of print, (one can occasionally purchase a second hand copy) they depict decorative ironwork that is breathtaking in design and execution, Many of the commissions shown were inspired by nature, designs incorporating birds, fish, plants and animals which, sculptured in iron, display a unique sense of humour and character. The ironwork of Fritz Khun has been and still is a major inspiration for amateur and professional smiths alike. I have seen many a good artist blacksmith try to reproduce examples of Fritz Khun's work; however, in my opinion no one has yet achieved his mastery of the craft.

Eric, our metalwork teacher, also taught electronics. He instigated many excellent projects in school that were on the cutting edge of technology at that time. A small group of us manufactured a two manual with pedal board electronic organ that played for assemblies in the school hall for at least fifteen years. Had I been more successful in mathematics, I could possibly have made electronics my career. I spent much of my time tinkering with radio sets, wiring up amplifiers and other electrical devices. In the metalwork room at school, I designed and made a tape recorder deck that actually worked; in fact, the project, guided of course by our teacher, won an award at a regional educational exhibition of science and technology.

I made room in the small wooden shed at the side of our house to accommodate a bench on which I could use my soldering iron and assemble electronic components for the projects I had in mind. I repaired radio receivers for family and friends and built a powerful amplifier, much to the annoyance of our neighbours who complained ceaselessly regarding the loud music emanating from the shed. One afternoon I ran two thin wires from the amplifier in my electronic hut to a loud-speaker that I hid behind a bush in the front garden of a house fifty yards down the road. I repeated this exercise taking two more wires to a second loud speaker hidden within the rockery of a front garden two houses further up the street. A switch enabled the individual connection of each speaker to my amplifier and microphone.

Electronic Antics

All being ready, I peered through a spy hole at the front end of the shed and waited patiently until my first victim, a middle aged man, happened to walk by the first speaker. 'Hello', I spoke into the microphone, 'Hello', came the reply and the guy turned to see who had spoken. A look of complete bewilderment enveloped his face as he stood staring into space. Quickening his pace he continued along the road during which I switched over to the other speaker. 'Hello', I greeted the puzzled commuter, 'Are

11

you well?' Our friend again turned to reply and once again seeing no one there ran up the road as if to escape the supernatural. A short while later, a group comprising two young couples were strolling along the footpath and as I observed them passing one of the hidden speakers, I dropped a number of coins onto the floor in close proximity to the microphone. Upon hearing the sound of coins rolling about on the floor, both couples immediately froze before searching diligently for the money that had been dropped and checking their pockets in order to discover who had lost what.

Through out my life, I have enjoyed situation comedy; as a child I laughed hysterically at the television programme; 'Candid Camera', watching poor unsuspecting individuals being set up in order to humour the viewing public. I have often found laughter therapeutic in times of difficulty and distress, perhaps I would have made a better comedian than a blacksmith, though I have often enjoyed trying to be both.

Occasionally, during the school holidays, myself and a couple of school friends would arrange a day walking in the Peak District, travelling on board the Nottingham to Manchester X2 coach, before alighting at our starting point of discovery with the eagerness and intrepidation of explorers into the unknown. I found the scenery awesome, the steep hills appeared as huge mountains, limestone cliffs seemed impossible to scale, rivers sped through huge canyons and danger lurked everywhere. To the impressionable mind of a twelve year old, such overwhelming scenery totally captivated the imagination.

Eventually, metalwork became one of my A level subjects, in which I designed and made a hand forged pair of gates as part of the coursework. At that time, I also had acquired a Saturday job helping Tom in his forge, where he allowed me to make fire irons and basic items such as hooks and staples, etc. I cut steel bar into lengths for forging horseshoes, he paid me four shillings for a days work. I could have earned more working in the local greengrocers, however, I enjoyed the forge much better; it just seemed the natural place for me to be.

Once, we took part in a combined family outing with our parents in visiting the Bakewell show, a long established country event in an idyllic rural setting. I happened to be fourteen years old at the time and by now had been helping Tom in his forge on numerous Saturdays. At midday, as we sat down to enjoy a packed lunch that Mother had provided, I observed a blacksmith demonstrating a portable forge powered by a hand driven blower. I immediately ran over to watch him forging a 'Derbyshire Ram's Head poker'; it happened to be the first time I had seen one being made and mentally recorded every process. Back at school I asked my metalwork teacher if I could make one and sure enough Eric obliged, proceeding to talk me through the processes required. The finished poker appeared to be a reasonable piece of work. It astounded Tom, who in turn asked if I would teach him how to make one!

Our local blacksmith, Tom, spoke in broad local dialect, which today would require an interpreter for anyone to understand what he was saying. Occasionally, and especially when I visit the area of my childhood, I sometimes hear old stagers talking in the same manner, it is music to my ears! D H Lawrence wrote a poem in this dialect entitled 'The Colliers Wife', the poem relates the moment every miners wife dreaded; news that her 'Mesta had got ot at t' pit'. One of my school chums, later in life, published a book entitled 'E up ma duck', about the local mining community and its dialect; he relates the tale about an old Ilson (Ilkeston) fella taking his cat t'vet, 'Iv cum ta sey ya baht ma cat'. 'Oh yes sir, is it a Tom?' 'Nay yoth, av got t' bugger aht sade in cewa'.

My Grandfather (adopted side) had worked all his life as a miner and some of my earliest memories are of him arriving home from work as black as the coal he mined. I remember my Grandmother taking two huge copper kettles of boiling water from the living room range to the kitchen and empty them into a tin bath; she would then help to scrub her husband's back before making his snap or packed lunch for the next day.

Today I am still haunted with vivid memories of my childhood, images of places and events from the past frequently resurrect themselves in my mind as if they had only happened yesterday. Although we were an ordinary working class family, struggling to make ends meet as our country endeavoured to rebuild its dignity in the post war period and food essentials were still rationed, somehow we never went hungry. Mother's careful thrift and monetary planning ensured we were respectably fed and clothed, even managing to save for an annual seaside holiday.

Our Sundays were devoted to Church and worship, though the preparation and cooking of a full Sunday lunch became an important task not to be missed. During the rest of the week, we frequently had lunch at Grandmothers house, as she happened to live conveniently close to my school.

Most of our vegetables were home grown, My Grandmother seemed to have been endowed with 'green fingers,' possessing an extraordinary talent in matters horticultural. She lived in a neat, rented Edwardian terraced house having both front and back gardens. A covered passageway provided access to the back yard, shared with the house next door. To the rear of this cobbled area, her back garden stretched as a twenty foot wide strip of land for some two hundred feet. The garden happened to be a treasure trove of fruit, flowers and vegetables which provided our daily requirements throughout the year. Her pantry which had also served as an air raid shelter during the war was accessed down a flight of eight stone steps under the stairs, it contained innumerable jars of preserves, pickles, potatoes and home grown vegetables that were stacked neatly on the cool stone shelves. This items provided many a makeshift meal as and when required.

My Grandfather maintained a chicken run and hen shed situated at the bottom of the garden. This regularly supplied us with the eggs laid by a number of hens who resided within. Occasionally one of the birds would be killed and dressed in order for his wife to prepare a special Sunday lunch when other relations were invited to join us for the meal.

Grandfather, an extremely tall, grey haired man in his late fifties, enjoyed smoking pipe tobacco, he always had his pipe visible, either in his hand or his mouth. He wore a shirt without a collar and a waistcoat sporting a silver pocket watch and chain. His attitude to children was that little boys should be seen and not heard, I was not therefore permitted to speak at the meal table whenever Grandfather was present, other than to ask politely if the salt could be passed. I also had to eat everything on my plate otherwise whatever was left, would be served to me the following day, cold of course!

Grandfather had lost three fingers during a mining accident and was now employed caring for the donkeys who pulled the wagons of coal at the bottom of the pit. My adoptive mother, his only daughter, had five brothers and upon the rare occasions when the whole family and all their grandchildren were together, the house was bursting at its seams.

The house had no electricity, its main light being a gas mantle mounted above the dining table. Grandma, however possessed an early valve radio in a huge walnut cabinet. The receiver was powered by a pair of large batteries in glass containers containing sulphuric acid, which were called accumulators and they frequently had to be charged at the local garage and hardware store. Transportation of these batteries could therefore be a risky business if they were broken or damaged.

In many ways we had a healthy life style, our home-grown fruit and vegetables were seasonal and fresh, walking and cycling happened to be our main method of transport where short distances were involved. The roads were relatively uncongested, community spirit prevailed and neighbours were neighbours in the real sense.

Forging iron became an addiction, unfortunately when I commenced a three year teacher training course at St Andrew's College, studying design in wood and metal, my education in the craft of forgework came to an abrupt halt, even though the college workshops had limited blacksmithing facilities, including a forge-hearth installed in what once had been an old outside lavatory. The metalwork lecturer, whose speciality was silversmithing, argued that the teaching of blacksmithing was irrelevant in craft education and refused to accept that his critique of my craft also applied to the traditional techniques of silversmithing that he practiced. My specialisation at college therefore, concentrated upon the design and manufacture of furniture, learning the techniques of woodcarving, cabinet making, woodturning and sculpture.

During the college holidays, I acquired a temporary job working for a firm of family joiners and undertakers. Whereas the pay could have been much better, I found the practical experience extremely useful and learned much that was to help me in my work at college. One morning, I arrived to find a coffin lying upon two trestles in the centre of the workshop. The oak coffin appeared to contain a body that had been collected the previous evening, though the face could not be seen, being shrouded in a large piece of cloth. 'Where did that come from?' I enquired of the foreman who had emerged through the door. 'The body came in last night, the poor fellow had a heart attack, though had lived to a good old age'.

I resumed my work, cutting the tenon joints for a number of work benches that had been ordered for our manufacture. 'Where is Ian?' I enquired. 'It's not for him to be late!' 'He won't be in today,' replied the foreman, 'as he is suffering from cold and flu'. Ian happened to be the firm's apprentice, who had so far worked for the firm for nearly two years. I returned to proceed with my work, when all of a sudden, with a large groan, the body in the shroud sat up!! I uttered a huge scream and fled to the other side of the workshop. My heart had suddenly begun to impersonate the huge bass drum of a symphony orchestra performing the Eighteen Twelve Overture! To coin a phrase, everyone came out of the woodwork laughing hysterically, including Ian who climbed from out of the coffin!

When I eventually began my short teaching career in the city of Nottingham, again I happened to be thwarted in practicing and teaching forgework. The head of the craft department suffered from acute asthma and totally banned the use of the forge, due to the fumes that invaded the workshop. It seemed curious however, that Frank seemed quite happy to spend his extended breaks and lunch hours in a staff room fogged and heavy, with the cigarette smoke of staff seeking acute psychological relief from the trauma of the class room jungle.

Three years on and successful opportunities happily came my way at another school; at last I became my own boss, having the opportunity to organize my own schemes of work. Forge-work now became an important ingredient of the metalwork syllabus, especially as I had been fortunate at that time to have the opportunity to attend training courses in forge-work skills. I remember in particular a week spent learning aspects of the craft at West Dean College in West Sussex. Our tutor, specialized in forged metal sculpture and whereas I initially had every intention of learning more traditional techniques, such as various scroll endings, leaves and twists, upon seeing this sculptural work in forged iron, my eyes were opened to a new world in blacksmithing and with no holds barred, I launched into such a journey of discovery that it became the basis of my work in iron for my future career. I will, of course, never forget the horrendous tube and railway connections returning home after the course, carrying my personal luggage plus two hundred weight of forged sculpture.

Shortly after, I was privileged to attend the first international conference in forging iron at Hereford college and took the opportunity to join the newly formed British Artist Blacksmiths Association , (BABA). At that time the smiths who specialized in decorative iron work were divided into two distinct camps; those who practiced work solely of a traditional nature producing ironwork in the designs of yester-year and a new breed of artistic smiths who wished to move the craft forward into the present century, with work of a contemporary nature. I remember the seminars and discussions that developed into heated verbal exchanges between these two schools of thought; the pure traditionalists maintained the craft of good decorative blacksmithing was being destroyed, that bludgeoning a piece of steel under the power hammer and daring to call it art was not their view of forge-work. The contemporary school argued however that new skills and techniques were being discovered, leading to designs that would easily marry up to a more modern architectural style; whereas, the traditionalists were only serving to fossilize the craft.

As future years were to prove, the experimentation in style and technique achieved by this new breed of smiths has certainly borne fruit and in my opinion extremely high standards of work have been maintained. Today's Artist Blacksmiths take great pride in using the heat of the forge to create their work and using many traditional techniques to create contemporary designs. At the conference, my eyes were opened further, I saw some of the best creative minds of blacksmithing in action. I came away inspired, enthused as never before, fired up and ready to go, only to be brought down to earth with the lack of opportunity to realize my true ambition to become a smith.

Eventually and thoroughly disillusioned with the gradual disappearance of the 'hands on involvement' in craft education, in favour of the 'academic approach', I decided to make the break from teaching and commenced working for two years with a local village blacksmith named Ben, whose forge was situated alongside the village pub, that incidentally had provided him an available watering hole when refreshment was required and to Ben that never was often enough!

Chapter 2
The spark is kindled

Ben was a general purpose smith whose work ranged from the shoeing of horses to the repairs and maintenance of machinery belonging to the local farmers; he also applied himself to producing various items of domestic and decorative ironwork. His workshop was extremely untidy, in fact it became a mountaineering trek to walk from one end of the building to the other, having to clamber over piles of tractor spares, vehicle parts, old horseshoes, forged harrow teeth, and hundreds of items collected during a lifetimes work. Ben would seldom discard any item as scrap, 'it will always come in fa sumat' he'd remark before making a further attempt to light his pipe.

On one occasion I remember an elderly chap entering the forge asking if we could help him repair a magneto for an ancient motorcycle whose manufacturer had long since gone out of business. 'A mite be able ta help tha theer' replied Ben, 'that's if a knows the pile it's unda'! He then clambered into a corner of the workshop and began to explore a huge mound of jumble. Sure enough, after searching diligently for about ten minutes and with a huge grin of achievement, Ben happened upon an old musty and decaying cardboard box containing an unused magneto of the same type.

We spent most of our time in the workshop re-forging the iron tines on the traditional drag harrows the farmers towed with their tractors, in order to rake their fields after the initial ploughing and before sowing the seed. The basic design and the manner in which they were bolted to the main frame had not changed since the days of the heavy shire horses that were eventually replaced by modern mechanical methods of towing. There were normally two varieties of harrow teeth, the pointed and the duck's foot. Usually when the pointed harrow teeth were too worn to be re-forged, a small blade of iron or steel was fire-welded on to the end giving the tine the appearance of a duck's foot. The pointed tines were called seed harrows and broke the ground into finer particles, the duck's foot harrows were used to break heavier soils and clay.

Fire-welding is one of the ultimate skills of the smith; the ability to heat two pieces of iron or steel in the forge fire and place them together upon the anvil at white heat whereby they would be welded into one piece by hammering together. We normally commenced the re-forging of harrow tines at the beginning of November, giving us enough work through to March. Many of the tines were virtually welded to their frames with rust, and therefore the removal of the large square nuts that held them in place presented difficulties in the extreme. Ben had a few tricks up his sleeve which made the job easier; hammering a chisel hard on two sides of the nut expanded the hole and nine times out of ten the nut would unscrew, failing this, heat applied with a gas torch would normally become the final solution. In recent years the traditional harrows have been superseded with bought in heavier replaceable tines, and due to the evolution in modern farming machinery, the re-forging of harrow teeth is now seldom undertaken by the blacksmith today.

Ben had won a place on the local district council serving as an independent candidate; he had a tremendous personality, a great sense of humour and had been trained as a blacksmith in the steelworks before taking over the forge after the sudden death of his father a few years before. Due to his daytime commitments with council work, Ben often left me to soldier on in the forge by myself. I therefore had to deal personally with many of Ben's customers, trying to pacify impatient farmers who had expected their repairs to have been completed weeks before. Indeed there was no hurrying Ben, he would gossip to anyone who passed by and sometimes it seemed as if time did not exist, he would even natter quietly and for ages on end to the horses that were brought to him for shoeing.

I personally have never had any inclination to be a farrier, it has not interested me one little bit! Someone once asked me how I would shoe a horse and replied, 'Shoo!, Shoo!, Shoo!' Ben however had a natural way with the equine species, I have seen him calm an unruly or lively beast by a successful combination of Polo mints, stroking behind the ear and a half hour spent in quietly muttering nonsensical utterances whilst continually looking the horse in the face .

One of Ben's neighbours often visited the forge; Derek had the appearance of a large pot bellied garden gnome, having a head crowned with a huge area of bald wasteland and a short pointed beard protruding from his chin. He had been a friend of Ben for a great many years, in fact both had been school mates in their youth and a bond of comradeship had survived throughout their acquaintance. Derek had taken early retirement from the fire service, his main interest being gardening and in particular the maintenance of an immaculate lawn, which extended for at least an acre round the front of his house. Derek spent a large proportion of his time mowing the grass, in fact he shaved his lawn to the specifications of the putting greens to be found at some top professional golf courses. I remember one particular hot summer during which a hose pipe ban happened to be in force and all the other lawns in the village were parched and brown; Derek's pride and joy happened to have the colour of a snooker table and the texture of velvet. Rumour had it that late at night, when the village quietly slumbered and the church clock struck twelve, as the owls screeched and hooted, a phantom shadowy apparition emerged in the guise of Derek wielding a hose pipe, in order to shower droplets of the elixir of liquid life to the thirsty shoots of his lawn.

Derek had a part time job, working behind the bar in the local pub; he happened to be a popular, jovial person who always enjoyed a joke, especially if the joke happened to be on someone else. Often at closing time he would inform the last customer that the police were outside inquiring as to the out of date tax on their vehicle parked outside on the road. As soon as the worried individual rushed outside to face the alleged music, Derek would lock the door and close the pub for the night.

One fine spring day, I had an idea and drove into town, before the supermarket closed, to purchase three punnets of mushrooms and a bundle of cocktail sticks. At twelve thirty that evening when Derek had

Mushroom Geometry

retired to his bed, Ben and I carefully planted the mushrooms by means of the cocktail sticks, in circles, triangles, squares and circles within circles throughout the front of Derek's lawn. In fact our exercise in horticultural geometry became a work of art.

The following morning Derek opened the front door to pick up his morning milk delivery. He stood mystified, amazed and bewildered at the sight of his front lawn; how on earth could this happen overnight? Gingerly he ventured onto the lawn taking great care to avoid treading on any one of the many mushrooms that had magically appeared, what would happen to him if he dared to venture inside any one of these shapes? Eventually upon seeing the Christmas tree fairy placed inside one of the mushroom circles planted near the edge of the lawn, did Derek begin to realize that he had been set up and remembering the date, April the first, he shouted; 'OK show your face you b'stards, it's mushroom soup for supper!'

Ben and his wife, Barbara, lived in a small Victorian terraced house some half mile distant from the forge, they had one unmarried daughter Patricia in her early twenties, who lived at their home and worked as a secretary in a local government office. Ben's main interest was the restoration of a steam traction engine situated at the bottom of his garden, he became so busy with his work as a district councilor that he failed to give the steam engine the attention required and it lay in a sad neglected state| covered with a green canvas tarpaulin. Ben had a short stocky appearance with slightly hunched shoulders, his large face had many architectural features such as a massive canopy of bushy eyebrows that would shelter his ruddy cheeks from any kind of inclement weather the elements would throw at them; on many occasions he would use a huge muscle in his forehead to lift his left eyebrow nearly to the height of his receding forelock, therefore displaying the most quizzical expression I have ever seen.

I persuaded Ben to join the Blacksmiths' Association and attend their annual conference in Sheffield. The cost of £50 covered meals and accommodation over a three day period. There were talks and demonstrations by smiths of international reputation, exhibitions of work, items of second hand equipment for sale and the annual competition that was to make a useful item of our own choosing from one piece of flat bar eighteen inches long, within the space of an hour. Ben asked me if I was entering, I replied that I would only make a fool of myself, being so inexperienced; however as I sat and watched the others taking part, I began to consider having a go.

A design of a contemporary set of four coat hooks came to mind; donning my leather apron I found a forge hearth that no one happened to be using and set to work feverishly hammering away. I completed my design just as time was called for me to stop working. When all the other contestants had completed their pieces, the numerous entries were laid out upon a table for the judging to take place by the overseas guest demonstrator.

We all held our breath as the first prize was announced and I could not believe that he had chosen mine as the winning piece. Although the £50 prize I received paid for the cost of attending the conference, the greatest reward for me happened to be the confidence I had gained in knowing that I had within me the ability to become a true blacksmith after all.

Some weeks later I arranged a meeting with the County's Arts Officer in order to introduce myself and discover the opportunities that were available to young aspiring artists and sculptors at the beginning of their career. Her eyes lit up when I showed her the coat hooks I had made; she asked if I would consider selling her the piece of work. She paid £25 for the coat hooks and it seemed that I had yet again overcome another milestone in my journey into the craft.

One spring morning, at the beginning of March, I arrived at the forge early to find that Ben had lit the forge fire in anticipation of shoeing a pony named Pythagoras, owned by the teenage daughter of a solicitor, who lived in the Old Manor House at the end of the lane by the Church. Elisabeth happened to be a spoilt youngster who was given every material wish she desired. We called her 'Loud Lizzy' as she was well known in the village for her frequent tantrums and the cheeky manner displayed when she could not have the attention she required. Ben always insisted that lively horses and ponies were well exercised before they were brought to him for shoeing and Lizzy had been told to do this with her pony, who was known to exhibit similar outbursts of mood swings to that of his owner. Observing the lively nature of the animal, Ben asked Elizabeth if it had been exercised that morning, Lizzy retorted she had been riding him for about an hour, a statement that could not have been further from the truth.

As usual Ben fed the pony a few Polo mints and proceeded to talk to him in hypnotic dulcet tones for some time. Elizabeth however became extremely impatient, complaining to Ben in her abrupt loud manner that her day was planned out and she had not taken into account Ben wasting her time trying to impersonate Dr. Dolittle! I personally did not see the pony kick Ben into the forge door, as I was inside and making sure that the two horseshoes in the forge fire were kept at an even temperature. Ben happened to be one of the old school of farriers who hot shod all of his horses and hand forged all of his shoes. I heard the incident however and ran out to see Ben lying upon the floor and Elizabeth screaming and chasing down the road in order to catch Pythagoras, who being startled had broken away from his tether. Ben was in great pain and unable to stand on his feet. I therefore called an ambulance which took him to the local Hospital and after numerous tests, the diagnosis revealed Ben having two slipped discs in his spine; he spent two of the following months unable to walk and had to sleep on a board. It was four months before Ben appeared at the forge and a further two months before he was able to completely resume his work.

I now became the full time bread winner taking on more work of an architectural nature as I was unable to practice as a farrier. I manufactured a pair of trestles in order to assemble iron gates in a civilized fashion and not on the floor outside the forge as Ben happened to do. First of all however, I had to make room for them in the forge, tidying the numerous piles of artefacts that littered the floor; in fact I had become uncertain that a floor actually existed as I had never set eyes on it so far and with clients arriving at the forge to discuss ironwork of a domestic nature, I had become embarrassed at bringing them to what must have appeared to have been a scrap yard from Hell!

Operation clean up commenced without Ben's knowledge, it was intended to be a pleasant surprise when he eventually returned, however the task presented a far greater challenge that I first thought and I also realised it was more than my life's worth to throw anything away. Ben had however, several large units of rusty steel shelving that had lain overgrown with huge bushes of vicious stinging nettles outside at the back of the forge. Risking therefore being stung to death, I carefully rescued the shelving units that had originally been bought from a sale of factory equipment and proceeded to clean them with a wire brush and finally coating the shelves with metal primer.

The cleaning up operation was performed after work in the evenings, I categorized the shelving into farriery, farming equipment, harrow teeth, auto parts, electrical, tools, paint, reference books, catalogues, forming jigs, nuts, bolts, and screws, rivets, hinges, chain links and hundreds of items that did not seem to fit into any particular compartment. The task became a nightmare, eventually however, portions of an ancient cobbled floor began to see the first light of day for years and three weeks later Ben's forge was unrecognisable from its previous condition. I even whitewashed the walls; the place had become clinical in the extreme.

During the clean up operation, I requested the local folk who came to the forge in Ben's absence, to refrain from telling him what we had done. I wished to keep it a surprise for his return, though the many folk who knew Ben well did not seem to think it was a good idea. 'If aw wa they' exclaimed one farmer, 'Ard tey ta tha hills afore Ben can catch they'!

Ben's absence allowed me to undertake a commission for my first sculptural gate intended for a house overlooking the sea front. A girl friend at that time had introduced me to a fascinating book called; 'Jonathan Livingstone Seagull', written by a flight engineer and made into a film set to music by the singer Neil Diamond. The book relates the story of how a young seagull, not content with the daily humdrum life of diving for fish, enjoyed flying high and learning aerobatic manoeuvres. On one occasion he gave the flock an impressive display of his flying skills, culminating in a steep dive from a great height down through the flock, finally banking out close to the surface and returning to the other gulls. Jonathan expected acclaim and admiration, unfortunately he was only to receive severe admonishment as the Elders of the flock regarded the dive as an act of gross stupidity exclaiming 'You could have collided and killed another gull'. The book contains impressive photographs of flying gulls silhouetted against the early evening sky which provided the inspiration of the forged images contained in this gate. Even today I still regard this gate as one of my finest pieces of work, perhaps the huge amount of enthusiasm in my early years had won where technique and experience were lacking.

Ben's friend, Derek, often visited the forge and proved a great help as and when required; his ability to strike heavy blows with a sledge hammer enabled work to be completed more quickly. Derek also helped in the

The Jonathan Gate

Too tidy for words

tidying up of Ben's workshop though happened to be unsure whether we had made the correct decision.

The day came for Ben's return to the forge and like Jonathan Livingstone Seagull, I too expected praise and acclaim for my inordinate efforts. Ben entered the building pipe in his mouth and suddenly stood perfectly still, his face looked aghast, his knees began to tremble, the pipe dropped from his mouth and broke on the floor, his bushy left eye eyebrow leapt so high it nearly fused with his hair. A faint indecipherable muttering became evident which grew louder to a roar of WHY?! Then silence as he walked around the room with his eyebrow still elevated, scrutinising every shelf as if performing a mental stock take. One could have cut the atmosphere with a knife, 'What would you have me do?' I stammered 'Have left the F**kin place as it was?' Ben replied 'Asl neer eva bey able ta feind owt narr'. Ideas were coming to mind to empty the neatly stacked shelves back into piles on the floor and as the weeks drew on the piles again began to grow, I can't remember Ben ever placing any article back on those shelves.

He never forgave me for tidying the forge, I realised that one of his pleasures in life happened to be searching to find; a lifetimes searching had given him endless pleasure and who was I to deny him of this? Ben however happened to be extremely impressed with the gate I had made and before it left the workshop he would proudly show it to everyone that came by.

Eventually after two years of working with Ben, the time had come for me to find my own forge; the flames of my career in blacksmithing were about to be lit.

Chapter 3
The fire is lit

I was given the opportunity to demonstrate a forge in a local museum one Sunday afternoon, the forge had been created to resemble an old village blacksmith's workshop complete with a set of circular double acting bellows, anvil, side bench and leg vice. The small room was on view to the public who stood watching the demonstrations from the adjacent corridor and behind a plastic screen.

Upon the anvil lay a hammer donated by the widow of Percy Joyston, the late blacksmith of Moslingham, a small village near the coast. Percy had been born in the village, having continued his father's trade as blacksmith and wheelwright until the age of seventy four, whereby the cataracts on his eyes had prevented him from working the forge any longer. Little was I to realise that one day I would be working full time in Moslingham forge, hammering away at the very same anvil that had served Percy well for a lifetimes work. I recollect having watched Percy demonstrating his craft at a country show many years earlier, he was using this hammer, recognisable by the extremely thin portion of the wooden shaft at the place where it was held. The cutlers of Sheffield had similar shafts on their hammers, they were deliberately whittled to a thin section in order to give the tool a whippy feel, thereby helping to achieve a quicker hammering action, keeping the thin blades hot for a longer period of time. Rapid blows will actually preserve the heat within a thin piece of steel. I remember once meeting one particular character at a blacksmiths' convention, who would commence hammering a thin steel nail from cold in such a rapid manner that he would make the end red hot in order to light a cigarette. This became his party piece, performed to amaze his audience, just as Percy would relate how a lifetimes blacksmithing had resulted in his hand gradually wearing away the shaft of his hammer to its present condition. Unfortunately the hammer happened to remain too sacred an object for me to use during my demonstrations at the Museum; I therefore placed the item upon the side bench prior to commencing my working of the forge that afternoon. If I had broken the hammer's thin shaft I would never have been forgiven!

The forge fire, lit from paper and sticks began to take hold as the bellows were steadily pumped. On this occasion I happened to be burning coal, not coke, as a ready supply was available having been provided for the steam traction engines which were occasionally fired up outside in the museum yard. The corridor quickly filled with visitors eager to see what was happening, which became exceedingly difficult as dense smoke decided to invade the room rather than exit up the chimney. The forge had obviously been built more from an aesthetic standpoint rather than with practical and ergonomic considerations in mind, in fact this happened to be one of the most useless chimneys I have ever seen. The room and corridor were now completely fogged and with twenty or more onlookers coughing and spluttering, almost choking in the

Smoked out

31

smoke, I gave up pumping the bellows and retreated with everyone else in order to breathe fresh air from outside. I abandoned the afternoon's demonstration, leaving the museum's technician to probe the flue in order to find out if there happened to be a blockage of any kind preventing the chimney removing the smoke. It was only then that he discovered to his surprise that a family of starlings had nested in the chimney for several generations.

After the chimney was swept and a canopy installed I began to demonstrate forge-work at the museum regularly on Sunday afternoons. The chimney seemed to work but only when the wind outside blew from any direction except the North East, upon whence frequent gusts of smoke blew out into the room sending visitors scurrying away from the scene. My demonstrations however seemed to be popular and many small items such as pokers and toasting forks were sold to those who stayed to watch me work. I also began to obtain orders for larger items such as fire-grates, traditional lighting and weather-vanes to be made with Ben at his forge.

Travelling the fifteen mile journey to the museum forge on one extremely foggy Sunday morning, I took a wrong turning and headed along a road that led into unfamiliar territory. Eventually I became lost and stopped alongside a single house at the side of some woods in order to ask anyone there for redirections. Little was I to realise that stopping here would also result in the redirection of my future career! The house, I noticed, had long curved bars of black forged iron attached to its white painted walls. Its massive garden housed a long wooden shed having a round steel chimney protruding from the end wall. Surrounded by countryside and woods, the silence was broken by a familiar sound, the ring of a hammer striking steel, music that had become the regular accompaniment to my daily work. The gate bore a wooden sign bearing the words; 'Alex Thompson Artist Blacksmith', I glanced into the sky wondering whose hand had guided me here?

Alex's wife opened the door she seemed a small cheerful soul and gladly explained the nearest way into town. After asking her if I could meet Alex, she led me to his workshop and upon opening the door the hammering stopped as the blacksmith looked up to see who had arrived. Occasionally I have met smiths who have resented any intrusion from whom they regard as a competitor who would profit from stealing their secrets. Alex however was the antithesis of the species and on learning that I earned my living in the same manner as himself, suggested that his wife made a pot of tea, inviting me to join him at the house for one almighty chinwag.

Alex had taken up blacksmithing on retirement from earning his living as a weather forecaster in the Royal Air Force, being self-taught in the craft apart from a one day's tuition by an expert from the then Rural Industries Bureau, now known as the Countryside Agency. Informing Alex that I happened to be demonstrating at the Museum's forge that afternoon, he asked if he might come along and suggesting that afterwards I join him and his wife for dinner.

Blacksmithing was more of a hobby to Alex than a full time business, he was fortunate in receiving a reasonable pension from the RAF. A number of small commissions had come his way therefore supplementing his main income. It quickly became obvious however that unlike many practising smiths, the craft had not taken its toll upon his physique. Alex happened to be a quiet, unassuming, well spoken, tall, slim, upright man wearing gold rimmed glasses. He appeared to be more suited to the boardroom than a blacksmith's forge. His wry sense of humour and quiet disposition added a beneficial eloquence and charm to the conversation of any group of people he met.

Compared to Ben's forge, Alex kept a workshop more in keeping with the operating theatre of the local hospital, tools were meticulously housed in pristine condition upon shadow boards attached to the wall. The anvil, forge canopy and larger tools were painted light blue, the floor was spotless. I'm certain that every ten hammer blows were interrupted by a severe sweeping around the anvil with a soft brush. I remember many years earlier Tom yelling at me to 'hit the hot metal and not to tickle it!' Alex certainly happened to be an expert in the latter, he would take twenty hammer blows to achieve what I could in two, in fact his hammer often fell as if attached to a parachute, gently landing in the required position, perhaps his RAF training contributed to this.

Alex had never received any form of Arts education, the very thought of using contemporary sculptural form as the basis for design disturbed his opinion of how forged ironwork should be produced. His experience in the craft had not progressed any further than the standard traditional motifs of previous centuries and although we were friends for many of the years that followed our style, concepts and approach were poles apart.

Shortly after our initial meeting Alex paid a visit to Ben's workshop and gazed in astonishment at the floor, now back to its original state covered in the heaps of this, that and the other, which had fast sprung up since the owner's return to work. That evening, chatting over a glass of beer at the local pub, Alex agreed that it was time for me to branch out on my own. I had now worked with Ben for two years and had to set up my own business if I were ever to gain a reputation as an artist blacksmith in my own right. He informed me of a small village forge, unused for a number of years, situated within his own parish and suggested that we investigate the possibility it serving my purpose. Alex seemed unconcerned however as to whether I would pose any threat to his own trade and certainly had no ambition to extend his business beyond the confines of his own workshop.

Sir Walter Beckingham-Smythe owned most of the village of Cupwood, whose limestone cottages were sheltered within a small valley surrounded by gentle rolling farmlands and meadows. The beautiful church with its tall graceful spire stood within the grounds of Cupwood Hall, a large seventeenth century manor house overlooking a beautiful lake. The village forge had indeed been disused for a number of years. It was an old stone building comprising the main forging area of some five hundred square feet and a 'shoeing shop' fifteen feet square. The forge, adjacent and joined to the village shop, had its double doors braced and secured by means of large padlocks attached to staples at each end of a long iron bar. The shopkeeper, a stocky jovial man in his early thirties, agreed to show us the interior of the forge currently being used as a temporary store for his boxes and bottles. The inside walls were still filthy with the dirt and grime of a blacksmith's shop and two massive oak beams, also covered in generations of soot, straddled the ceiling. The traditional stone hearth still contained the ashes of the last forge fire to be lit some fifteen years before, though the bellows had been removed in the years that followed. The shoeing room also had a massive wooden beam acting as a lintel for the two wooden doors and sure enough, stapled into the beam happened to be a large iron ring three inches in diameter. Smiths of yesteryear would use a rope threaded through this ring to elevate and immobilise the hind leg of an unruly horse and therefore create a safe situation for the animal to be shod, if only Ben had used this method with Pythagoras, his accident may never have occurred. Today a farrier may inject a difficult horse with a tranquillizer however the old blacksmith had to resort to more traditional methods.

Kevin, who ran the village shop, questioned the purpose of our visit; he knew Alex well and did not seemed surprised when asked if he would have any objection to the forge being used by an artist blacksmith. Kevin immediately replied that his trade could possibly benefit from the increased number of folk who would visit the forge. I had by now determined that Cupwood Forge would be the ideal premises in order to start my own business in blacksmithing and decided to apply to the Estate to lease the forge. Alex had a good knowledge of the administration of its farms, land and property; he agreed to arrange a meeting with Sir Walter, whom he knew from being a member of the local parish council.

A long established firm of land agents had been entrusted with the day-to-day running of the Cupwood Estate and after an initial and successful interview with Sir Walter, a representative from J.W. McCawley and Son arranged a meeting on site to thrash out the terms of a lease. I remember waiting nervously outside the forge at the appointed time as an olive green Range Rover drew up alongside the village shop.

Captain James McCawley, a tall distinguished individual, with a long angular face, sporting a short thin moustache embarked from the vehicle. Dressed immaculately in country attire, complete with Harris Tweed hat and jacket, he spoke with the authority of an ex-army officer, curt and to the point. Having obviously received a public school and military education, James had worked with the management of large country estates and their aristocracy since his retirement from the army some eleven years earlier. 'Are you the fellow I wish to see?' he asked, 'Well I guess we had better have a gander, can't say I've ever been in this place before, in fact never knew the blighter existed!'

The terms were agreed and two weeks later I received written confirmation of a short renewable lease relating to both the forge and to a small cottage in a nearby village. I had now to inform Ben about my intentions and make the preparations to move; my enthusiasm however being dampened by the breaking up of a long term relationship with my girlfriend Shirley, she would hear nothing of this venture; emotionally I was devastated.

Ben surprised me with his understanding, realising my career had little future at his forge, he gave the move his blessing and actually helped by donating a forge blower and a small anvil. Some three weeks later the old stone hearth in Cupwood Forge became filled with coke, the fire being lit with earnest intention.

Chapter 4
The flames take hold

Unlike the forge at the museum, my initial lighting of the fire proved a great success. The flames and smoke raced up the chimney with such an infectious eagerness and enthusiasm that I just could not wait to hammer away at the bar of steel I had placed into the fire. We were worried the original cast iron water tank at the rear of the forge would leak, owing to its age. The tank provided cooling to the air pipe or tuyere, therefore preventing it from burning away where the blast of air enters the fire. Fortunately the tank showed no sign of leaking and we knew the forge would work.

Traditional hearths of this type did not require a canopy, as flues and chimneys were constructed to the traditional formula of a twisted throat, increasing in aperture thereby creating a venturi effect that would suck the smoke up and out of the chimney. If only many of the builders in this day and age would learn from their predecessors, more of the flues that they build would work! The very first article I forged in this hearth happened to be a ram's head poker which I gave to Sir Walter and to this very day it has pride of place in the fireplace of the drawing room of Cupwood Hall.

Upon acquiring the keys to Cupwood Forge, I spent the initial days wire-brushing the walls and beams before painting the stonework white with cheap emulsion from the D.I.Y. The acquisition of all the associated tooling used in the daily operation of a blacksmithing business can be an extremely time consuming and expensive undertaking. Fortunately it is a craft where the majority of the hand tools used can be manufactured by the smith in his own forge. I have spent many Sunday mornings visiting local car boot sales, buying for a song countless hammer heads, chisels and tools that would easily be converted or reforged into useful items for the workshop. Large pincers for example are made of tool steel, they can be taken apart and re-forged into pointed scrolling pliers. Old builders' hammers can be transformed into leafing tools, the old box of chisels cleared out from under the bench of Grandad's old shed would provide an ideal source of steel in order to make the many punches, drifts and cutting tools required.

Time spent exploring car boot sales may often provide rich rewards especially as larger items such as anvils, leg vices, swage-blocks and heavier items of forging equipment occasionally surface among the heaps of bric-a-brac and domestic clearance displayed. Recently at a boot sale I came across a treasure trove of tongs, hammers, blacksmiths tools and an anvil in nearly new condition. They had been bought from a local school that had ceased to teach metalwork skills. 'How much are you selling these for?' I asked. 'Thirty five pounds' came the reply, 'Will you take twenty five?' 'Go on then!' answered the lady and my face never stopped smiling for the remainder of the day.

My savings in the bank were now gradually running out, steel, coke, paint, welding gas. the purchase of a second hand mechanical hacksaw, the installation of gas and electric welding equipment, all took its toll on the cash that I had available and I began to realise that unless I had some serious work commissioned, all my aspirations would turn pear shaped. Perhaps I had tried to achieve too much in too short a time!

Standing under the proverbial spreading chestnut tree would not bring in the work required and in order to achieve a profitable income I had to take the water to the horse. I had always been sincere in my belief that somewhere out there were folk willing to pay good money for my work and the question remained how the devil was I to find them?

I began to make more use of my demonstrations at the museum on Sunday afternoons, trying hard to possibly enthuse an available potential pot of customers and clients. The forge there had an audience of interested onlookers and I had to show folk that I could produce the goods; words alone would not merely suffice. I began to make a number of articles I could exhibit, smaller items such as fire baskets, candle-holders, sculpture and light fittings. Realising therefore, the design and execution had to be different to ironwork generally on sale elsewhere, it needed to be made to an extremely high standard of craftsmanship.

Work indeed began to materialise, mainly the smaller items such as those described, however on one sunny Wednesday morning an elderly couple visited the village forge. 'We watched you working at the museum last Sunday and took one of your cards', exclaimed the husband. The visitor, a seemingly intellectual, bespectacled man of medium height, became immediately recognisable by his short white beard and a head crowned with a large topping of snowy white hair. He wore a dark green wax jacket, brown corduroy trousers and introduced himself as Dr Broughton who lived in Honeysuckle Cottage at South Buscombe, a small village some nine miles distant. I have long since come to realise that many, if not all of our beautiful country villages have a clone of Dr Buscombe, a stereotype of the retired professional, living in his idyllic surroundings. The doctor now spent his time working as a parish councillor, being an active party member of the Lib Dems, a church warden and chairman of the village gardening club. His wife also played an extremely active role in the local community, running the W.I., the annual village fete and being well known as a leading authority in the making of preserves and home made pickles.

'We would like to commission you to make some traditional items for our inglenook fireplace', said Mrs Broughton 'Would you be able to pay us a visit?' 'We were impressed by your demonstration on Sunday afternoon!' echoed her husband, 'And are looking for a dog-grate, a set of fire irons and two wall lights, one for each side of the fireplace'. I arranged to visit their house early the following evening.

Honeysuckle Cottage indeed happened to be an idyllic double fronted Elizabethan stone cottage with pantiled roof and shuttered windows containing many small diamond panes of leaded glass. The property stood in the midst of large established orchard comprising all manners of mature fruit trees. A stream ran the full length of the front of the cottage before meandering through the adjacent water meadow and eventually disappearing towards the direction of the village church. A cobbled path provided access through the front garden to the house via a small rounded stone bridge over the stream. The old oak front door sheltered by an ancient porch overgrown by ancient ivy, housed two original iron strap hinges and a large Suffolk latch that were fastened to the wood by means of traditional hand-made nails. 'Would you prefer tea or coffee?' asked the doctor's wife, a small well rounded lady wearing a cotton check apron decorated by small pink squares, 'Or would you relish a glass of our home made rhubarb wine?' 'A nice cup of tea would be most welcome' I replied, as the grandfather clock in the hall chimed the hour of seven. Dr Broughton took me inside the lounge to show me the large, stone inglenook fire place that had been discovered recently upon the removal of a much smaller Victorian affair. 'We've had the chimney swept but not tested', he remarked.

Mrs Broughton appeared carrying a tray containing a small teapot, three china cups and a plateful of freshly baked scones complete with double whipped cream and homemade strawberry jam. 'We can't wait to have a fire in there' she said cheerfully, 'Now one sugar or two?'

The following day, I lit the forge fire and began to manufacture the ironwork that the doctor and his wife had ordered; the commission took me three weeks to complete. I began work usually at eight in the morning and apart from a short lunch break, worked through to around eight thirty in the evening. My enthusiasm to produce this work ran away with me, sheer determination drove me on until at last the day arrived when the items were delivered to Honeysuckle Cottage. I had burnished and lacquered the ironwork in order to produce a natural finish, our famous and popular ram's head fire irons hung from the arm of a shepherd's crook stand. The fire dogs that supported the stretcher bars holding the basket in place each had a large ram's head termination in order to match the fire irons. I bolted to the wall a heavy back plate with a decorative riveted edge and fleur de leys motif in the centre and stood at the far end of the room to view the work in place. Unfortunately the double wall lights could not be placed into position until the electrician completed the wiring.

Dr Broughton, keen to light the fire, appeared with an armful of kindling and newspaper. He placed this carefully in the fire grate to which he applied a burning match, before adding a few small dry logs. The fire took hold and soon we noticed small wisps of smoke rolling out under the huge fireplace beam and into the atmosphere of the room. Unlike the chimney of my forge, many cottage fires were constructed in a totally different manner, the massive base of the chimney behind the large beam had been used for the smoking of cheese, bacon and other meats. Our forebears were obviously not in the least bothered about living in a smoky atmosphere!

I recommended that the manufacture and fitting of a canopy seemed to be the obvious solution and although it happened to incur more expense, the canopy could also become a feature making the fireplace look even more attractive. After some discussion with his wife and providing I would guarantee a smoke free room, Dr Broughton further commissioned a canopy and register plate in order to seal the roof of the inglenook, a fender for the hearth and a huge fire guard to protect the carpet from sparks. Four weeks later, the finished project looked magnificent and further more it worked exceptionally well! All of the smoke now drew up the chimney and the doctor and his wife were delighted. The canopy hanging from the register plate had curved sides, its base being surrounded by a burnished and riveted strip of forged iron that turned inwards for two inches in order to roll any wayward smoke back to the centre of the fire. The larger space above the entry to the canopy would cause the hot air to expand thereby increasing its draw. The design of this canopy has always worked well in a countless number of similar situations over the years in fact we are now experts in smoke busting and the manufacture of fireplace furniture.

Moving on from the successful completion of my first commission at Cupwood Forge and with confidence unparalleled to date, I decided to take the bull by the horns and employ a trainee, one on whom I could rely in order to produce work of the standard required. I advertised and interviewed a number of applicants ranging from school leavers to those made redundant or in semi retirement from industry. I found the situation frustrating; School leavers having had little or no experience in hands-on work in traditional crafts and men from industry, indoctrinated by the trade union movement with little thought for a performance related pay situation.

Eventually I telephoned the head of design and technology at the local secondary school and asked if he could recommend a school leaver who being practically orientated had the ability to think for himself and the motivation to achieve good results for his employer. Brian, whom he recommended came from academic parents, both his mother and father were teachers and though their son had below average academic GCSE results, his attempt at the practical test I gave him seemed promising. I therefore decided to offer Brian an apprenticeship in forge-work. My business began to grow, commissions were flooding in, the sheer variety of work meant never a dull moment; work occupied most of my time, though now I also had to decorate the cottage in which I was living.

The couple, who had moved into the cottage next to mine, suddenly found their Labrador dog had given birth to a litter of pups, whose father had been a collie owned by a nearby farmer. The pups were reared until the time to find them homes and one small rascal began to make a beeline for me each time I came anywhere near. They say that a dog will find its owner and therefore I ended up taking possession of an extremely cute light brown puppy who I named Clinker. She became a constant companion for fourteen years until her unfortunate death in a car accident.

Clinker's main passion however, happened to be the retrieval of objects thrown and had been mischievously taught to catch beer mats projected through the air by a certain unnamed frequenter of the local pub. Clinker would amuse all and sundry by carefully pawing one off the table and gently placing it at the feet of a nearby customer, sitting staring at the mat until it was thrown for her to catch. I will remember forever a certain evening when one of the villagers who eventually became bored and tired of repeatedly throwing the beer mat, placed the article upon the top of the upright piano that stood at one end of the bar. Clinker stood on her hind legs trying to reach it with her front paws running up and down the keyboard. Everyone in the bar was in stitches with laughter indeed it happened to be one of the funniest sights I had seen. At that moment, the landlord entered the bar and upon seeing the dog performing enquired as to what music she happened to be playing? 'Bach of course!' I replied. We all collapsed with hysterics!

My second commission followed in quick succession. My adoptive parents, having retired to the coast, happened to update their carpet supplier on how I became a self employed blacksmith and as to my progress to date. The man informed them that one of his clients

Johann Sebastian Bark

happened to be seeking a firm to manufacture an unusual staircase for a residence they were currently having built. I immediately followed up this information and one morning met a local wealthy businessman, who had recently sold a large complex of holiday homes on that part of the coast and had built a retirement property above a huge swimming pool, on the edge his former empire. The staircase he required happened to be an extremely grand affair, consisting of two opposing curved polished brass hand rails either side of hard wood steps, covering a skeleton of a heavy steel angle iron frame. The entrance to the staircase measured twenty feet across, sweeping with equal curves to a fifteen foot exit at the first floor. The solid brass hand rail measured three inches wide and had to be shaped and polished from rectangular section on site. The whole job presented a huge undertaking and being one to rise to a challenge, I accepted the commission and began the work.

I carefully planned every stage of the work, my specifications and calculations being checked and assessed by a professional structural engineer. The brass handrail had to be manufactured in sections, being blind bolted to the curved steel under-frame. I hired a hand held portable buffing machine in order to produce the final highly polished finish, the small random twists in the round supporting spindles being gilded with 22 carat gold leaf.

The staircase warranted a large proportion of the work taking place on site, which necessitated our portable anvil and leg vice being used as a temporary work station set up on the patio outside. One particular morning however, a disastrous occurrence happened that seemed to jeopardise the whole commission. I emerged from within the building to find my apprentice Brian, angle grinding a piece of steel and unwittingly showering the grinding sparks on to the expensive plate glass French windows of the lounge. Upon close inspection, I discovered the glass had now been etched with particles of abrasive grinding dust and steel. Thoughts immediately came to mind that any profit made from the commission would be soaked up by the cost of providing replacement glass. Furious at Brian's thoughtless actions I told him in no uncertain terms how fortunate I happened to be in having the opportunity to employ such an intelligent and considerate apprentice! Brash Anglo Saxon expletives however would not resolve the situation, therefore with an idea in mind, I stormed off to the local DIY to purchase a number of small razor sharp cutting blades and a tin of 'Brasso' metal polish. We spent the remainder of the day furiously using the steel blades in the manner that one would use a steel cabinet scraper in an effort to remove the foreign particles from the glass. The procedure appeared to work and after a final rubbing over with the metal polish, the glass doors appeared to be no worse for their experience.

Our clients returned at 6pm from their shopping trip to the city remarking, 'Have you had a good day, we're sure that you have been working hard by your appearance, however there doesn't seem to be much visual progress in the staircase since yesterday!!'

When finally completed, the magnificent staircase became the major interior feature of the house; the polished brass handrail gleamed resplendent, complementing the myriad of gold leafed mini twists that shone like stars in the upright supporting spindles.

Chapter 5
Fires Outside

I enjoyed and looked forward to my demonstrations at the museum on Sunday afternoons, gradually acquiring a unique and humorous patter as I described the processes performed. Those watching me work seemed enamoured with my performance. I seldom left the forge without having sold many of the items I had made. One of the onlookers once asked me if I would demonstrate my craft at a local country show that he had the privilege of organising, a proposition that I found worthy of consideration. I held a meeting with him at the forge during the week that followed, to discuss the arrangements and agreed to pay a pitch fee of twenty pounds for the one day event. I have however long since learned, that to bring half a ton or more of equipment to a show, demonstrate and entertain the public, should require myself charging a fee to the organisers of the event or at the very least receive free trade-stand place. I have in the past had many a verbal fracas with greedy show organisers who require a working blacksmith as an attraction and yet ask for him to pay an extortionate pitch fee.

I designed and made a small portable forge for the event that consisted of a quarter inch thick steel tray, measuring two foot square by four inches deep. The tray had detachable steel tubular legs and underneath a small steel pipe, through which air was blown by means of a small centrifugal electric fan from seven small holes in the base of the hearth. Although the temperature in the fire often exceeds 2000 degrees centigrade, the steel base of the forge is prevented from melting by the draught of air from underneath cooling it down. I loaded the forge, anvil, leg-vice, box of tools, items for sale and a market stall loaned from a friend into a trailer to be towed by my small van.

I set off early on the day of the show, allowing plenty of time to set up my stand and equipment. The cloudy sky precipitated a fine drizzle, which the radio forecaster had expected to clear away during the morning, as the emerging sun would burn away the gloom, therefore leaving a fine afternoon.

Arriving at the show ground, my vehicle immediately became stuck in the muddy quagmire of the gateway entrance being churned up by the constant heavy traffic into the site. Eventually a tractor came to my rescue, towing my van and trailer to a portion of dry elevated land towards the top of the field. I worked furiously for two hours setting up my stand and equipment before wandering over to the organisers' tent enquiring as to the provision of electricity that had been promised in order to operate the forge blower. Upon being informed that the organiser had forgotten my requirements for electricity, I was faced with the choice of either moving to a new location, or hiring a portable generator as my stand happened to be out of range from their electrical supply.

Arguing that it happened to be their responsibility to provide a generator proved futile and rather than dismantle my stand in order to set up in a new location, I paid a further ten pounds to the organiser before carrying his spare 3.5 KVA generator to where I had set up the forge. By the time I arrived back to the stall another stand had set up along side, though I failed to notice as to the nature of the articles sold.

A blacksmith friend had advised me to burn charcoal as the fire would keep burning during time spent between demonstrations. He advised me to pour a small quantity of water around the perimeter of the fire at regular intervals to keep the heat located at the centre of the hearth. I lit the coals that morning, with paper and sticks and supplied a gentle blast of air causing a large initial quantity of smoke to blow in the direction of my next door neighbour's stall, selling white lace undergarments and knickers. Loud shrieks of 'Put it out!', emanated from the adjacent stand and a portly lady having features that resembled a welder's striking plate

And knickers to you too!

immediately appeared, telling me in no uncertain terms that I had to move to a more isolated position where her stock would not be soiled by my filthy occupation.

Having now had my fill of everything being against me that morning I stood my ground and, risking being turned into a frog, informed her ladyship that moving a ton of steel and equipment would be a far more arduous task than the relocation of a small quantity of knickers. The foul tempered female immediately hurried away in order to offer much grief to the organiser who by now had begun to feel that the asking of a blacksmith to demonstrate at his show had not been a wise idea after all.

Small agricultural country shows are managed and run according to long established traditions, catering for specific sections of the rural community that generally stay within the confines of the areas allocated to their specific interest. The stockmen for example, spend the day grooming their prize cattle, sheep and pigs before the judging takes place. The equine fraternity are busy participating in events organised within the paddock. Farmers spend much of their time assessing the possible future purchase of a new piece of heavy machinery and how it will ultimately be paid for. Members of the general public however seem to wander aimlessly, Grandma looking for the toilet, Father the beer tent, children pestering for ice creams and Auntie Flo searching for a nice cup of tea.

The gates were now opened to the public, who eventually began to drift in the direction of the forge. A small group gathered round as I began to demonstrate one of my famous ram's head pokers. At last the day seemed to improve until an old farmer in the audience exclaimed in a loud rural dialect, 'Yarr no blarksmith!' I pretended to ignore him and continued to hammer away at my work. Again the old fellow exclaimed; 'Yarr no blarksmith, al tell ya, yarr no blarksmith at all!' Being now embarrassed by his facetious comments I ceased hammering and asked, 'Why in your opinion am I not a blacksmith?' Mr Wurzel with his expressionless stare replied, 'Cos a blarksmith shoes harrses and as you don't shoe harrses yarr no blarksmith!' 'These days a farrier shoes horses', I retaliated. The old fellow once again commented in his loud drawl, 'In my book a blarksmith shoes harrses,' 'always harrs don, an always will do!' He then spat upon the ground, hit his stick on the floor and turned to walk in the direction of the beer tent. Making every endeavour to appear undisturbed by the incident I proceeded with the making of the ram's head fire poker now reaching completion, when a small boy asked his mother as to what I happened to be making. 'Can't you see,' she replied, 'the man's making a horseshoe.' In total exasperation I held the finished item aloft, turned to the crowd and said; 'Has anyone ever seen a horse with one of these on his feet?'

A lady once asked me to explain exactly how an Artist Blacksmith earned his living. I replied that he painted pictures on horses hooves! For a moment the woman remained silent as she obviously thought on what I had said. 'Don't they quickly wear away?' 'Not really!' I explained 'As they use the hard wearing paint which is employed for road marking.' 'Who gets to see them?' the lady asked again. 'The farrier of course,' I replied, 'It cheers him up when trimming the horses hooves!' 'One learns something every day!' she exclaimed upon leaving our stand.

I am frequently asked many ridiculous questions today especially when I demonstrate my craft at country shows, however to many folk in this day and age a blacksmith is a rare phenomena, an anachronism, a figment of the past and therefore I have to pity the unenlightened. Here then are but a few comments and questions from the shows that I have recorded for posterity:

'Come here Henry and look at this funny man dressed up as a blacksmith'.
'Oh look, here's a barbecue, I think we'll have some sausages!'
'What do you do for a real living?'
'This is a craft that died out years ago!'
'Do you make everything out of horseshoes?'
'Are you using real metal?'
'Do you forge aluminium saucepans?'
'How many times a day do you set yourself on fire?
'Do your pokers really poke?

And the small boy watching a demonstration and seeing me bounce the hammer upon the anvil in order to keep ones rhythm when turning the steel over, said to his Mother, 'He's no good Mum, he keeps missing it!' Towards the end of the afternoon the clouds again began to gather. The fine drizzle returned and the groups of onlookers drifted away, furthermore the electric fan blowing the air into the forge gave up the ghost and my demonstrations came to an abrupt halt.

I continued manning the stall for the short time left, giving out business cards to those few members of the public expressing an interest in my work. Unfortunately few sales were made and therefore when the show ended, I loaded my forge and equipment on to the trailer and returned the generator to its owner. Dusk began to fall and I set off back to the forge, glad that the whole sorry fiasco was over. Eventually it became dark and as I continued my long drive home, I noticed the reflection of a blue flashing light in the wing mirror of my van. I pulled into a lay by, wound the window down and enquired, 'Is everything in order officer?' 'Is your trailer on fire?' asked the policeman. It happened that the draught of travelling had brought the charcoal fire alight and I must have appeared as a huge mobile Roman candle, hurtling along the road, sending a volcano of sparks in one huge stream behind me.

The following morning after I had unloaded all my equipment from the trailer, I proceeded to take stock of the show, as to whether or not it would be worth all the effort and hassle by participating in a similar event in the future. Feeling rather despondent, I proceeded to make myself a well-deserved cup of coffee when the telephone rang. 'Hello is that Mr Pope?' a voice enquired, 'We took one of your cards at the show yesterday and require a price for a pair of gates to be made for our house'. Several other orders followed, all from the show. The event had obviously been worth the effort after all!

When living and working in a rural situation one has to accept to a certain degree the philosophy and culture of its way of life; a philosophy determined by the land, its industry, customs and the all important role played by the seasons of the year. Those who migrate to the countryside from an urban situation often find the assimilation difficult and to a certain extent incomprehensible as rural folk have received their education and upbringing within the countryside environment. I am certain however that the hearts of country folk do not beat as fast as those of the city dwellers, their whole lifestyle is sustained by the gradual progress of nature and any race against time seems confined to the relatively short periods of planting and harvest when the crops have to be gathered in quickly, often battling against inclement weather.

The escalating price of property in country villages has necessitated an exodus of young people whose roots were once embedded in the countryside and are now having to find more affordable accommodation in the towns and cities. In stark contrast, houses that once were occupied by farm labourers and agricultural workers are now being sold at high prices to the new breed of professional city commuters and retirees, who have moved from the concrete jungle to so called 'idyllic' peace and serenity. Even large country estates are now discriminating between the haves and have-nots in favour of prestigious and expensive tenancies for their attractive cottages and property.

The farming industry is also presently undergoing radical change, especially with having to compete with the cheaper imports of grain and produce from areas such as Eastern Europe. In order to survive, small farmers are now having to either diversify into specialist organic produce or joining a co-operative with others in order to share the cost of the expensive equipment required. The increasing mechanisation of the farming industry with its heavy machinery, coupled with the reduction in man power has also helped to reduce the numbers of those whose soul and spirit were once part and parcel of our rural heritage. Most farms by now have their own large workshops and no longer require the skills of the country blacksmith and the majority of rural forges have long since become derelict resulting in the cessation of businesses which had served the farmers for generations.

The future of blacksmithing lay now in the hands of the artisan rather than the tradesman, a craft that had provided the backbone of farming for centuries had now become virtually redundant. In retrospect my move to reopen Cupwood Forge may not have seemed a good idea after all especially in the light of events that followed.

The house situated next door to Cupwood Forge, on the opposite side to the village shop stood empty. The rental required for the dwelling however happened to be far more than I could afford at that time. A lane ran between the forge and this double fronted property down towards a few stone cottages that had been built along side the village beck, a stream meandering from the lake of Cupwood Hall towards the open countryside beyond. One morning Captain James McCawley parked his Range Rover outside in order to show a prospective tenant around. The man turned out to be a stern faced individual of average height, dressed in a dark brown suit, hair parted to one side and wearing a small Hitler type moustache. The visitor stood for a few moments gazing in the direction of the forge with a penetrating stare.

Two weeks later Mr Grimbly and his wife moved in to Lavender House, having relocated from the city in order to enjoy the relaxing atmosphere of a quiet country village. Mr Grimbly had recently become a partner in the firm of 'Worston and Grumpsford' Chartered Accountants, henceforth to be known as 'Worston, Grumpsford and Grimbly'. Shortly afterwards I introduced myself to the new incumbent only to be asked if he really had to suffer the noise we were making on Saturdays and in the evenings.

I had an inkling that trouble could be brewing and some three weeks later noticed an attractive young lady wearing a council identification badge

51

holding a clipboard, walking in all directions around the forge. Shortly after, I received a letter from the district council stating that complaints had been made concerning the amount of noise emanating from the building. I was therefore requested to limit my hammering and noisy activities to between the hours of 9am to 6pm on weekdays and between 9.30am and 12 noon on a Saturday, otherwise the matter would be taken further. Little was I to realise how much my business would suffer if clients were to require work completed quickly using hours that exceeded the times beyond which I had been permitted to work!

Craft shows at this time were extremely lucrative, I therefore applied to exhibit as a demonstrating blacksmith at a well- known local craft market, held each year during spring and summer bank holiday weekends at a tourist location near to the coast. The market had a traditional flavour being held in conjunction with a folk festival of national renown. Morris dancers and folk groups brought in thousands of onlookers who frequently purchased hand-made items from the many craft stalls on view. A local farrier and blacksmith by the name of Tony Gillespey also worked a forge at this event, Tony however had no objection to my also having a stall and suggested that we were situated next to each other and alternate our demonstrations in order to make life easier. Apparently their lay a hidden motive in this cunning reasoning as Tony would now be able to escape at regular intervals to the bar with the intent of lubricating his throat as a relief from the fumes and dust of the forge.

I remember one occasion on the Monday of a particular sunny bank holiday weekend, when the craft market became packed with hundreds of tourists, holidaymakers and families enjoying a great day out. I had a huge captive audience jostling and eager to watch my demonstrations at the small open forge I had brought with me. As I furiously hammered my iron on the anvil, a loud voice interrupted and I glanced upward to behold a tall distinguished white haired lady wearing stylish green Wellington boots, an immaculate Harris Tweed country coat and bonnet to match.

'I say!' exclaimed the woman in an extremely loud aristocratic voice, as one of the three white Labradors that she held upon leash made to cock his leg upon the stand of my anvil. 'Please excuse Hector', the Lady remarked. 'He's only doing what canine chaps have to do!' I made a deliberate effort to avoid adverse reaction and simply gritted my teeth, hoping that neither Hector or his companions would contemplate a number 2 within my demonstration area. 'I say!' she remarked even louder, 'Do you make door knockers? I have been contemplating one for the oak front door of the Hall for many years and now I believe I have found the very person who can do the job!'

It quickly became obvious that I happened to be in the company of a person of high renown, her charisma and loud accentuated manner of speech drew an even larger crowd of onlookers, who now began to view her as the centre of attraction.

'Can you describe the type of door knocker you would deem suitable for the door of a seventeenth century country manor ?' the lady enquired. I humbly suggested that a large ram's-head motif might grace the entrance. 'And what would your account be if I were to award you the commission?' 'I would imagine the work would be in the region of sixty pounds', I replied. 'The lady of the manor asserted that she rather relished the idea, as the farms she owned on the estate all bred sheep and a ram's head design would be most in keeping! 'I say', she continued, 'It may be a good idea to order two of them, one for the front door and one for the back, would you prefer a deposit?'. Having then paid an advance of fifty pounds, her ladyship remarked even louder as the crowd of onlookers gawped in sheer amazement, 'Now you will make an excellent job of them, won't you?' As the bystanders waited for my reply with bated breath I looked up and remarked, 'Madame, you'll have the finest pair of knockers in the county!!'

My services as a demonstrating blacksmith were soon in demand. I therefore began to pick and choose the events which I had found to be most lucrative and financially rewarding. My investment in an eight foot square marquee together with hard wearing blue and white striped weatherproof covers had however been a costly affair, even though I had made the steel frame and heavy plywood table tops. The marquee had an open canvas lean-to on one side, under which I could hammer away upon my small anvil, keeping dry during showers of rain. My portable forge stood outside the lean-to for reasons of safety. The whole outfit appeared impressive; the travelling blacksmith's show had truly taken to the road.

Showing Off

Another investment had been the purchase of a small second hand caravan, for accommodation at shows, as many of the events I attended were in the London and South Eastern area of the country. Work materialised at many of the shows that I could not have found locally at that time, enough to keep myself and apprentice in work.

It was during this time that I met the young lady who was later to be my wife. I had taken a stand at the County Show within the Rural Development Marquee, the subsidised space had been made available for new craft businesses that had been set up within the space of ten years. I entered my display into the competition for the best craft stand at the show and also one specific piece of work for the decorative ironwork competition, as did my apprentice Brian. The subject of the competition that year was to design and make a decorative hanging basket bracket and out of some fifteen entries, Brian came first and I gained the second prize. Consolation came however with Cupwood Forge gaining the first prize for the best rural craft stand at the show. I recollect the presentation of the prizes by the Princess Royal who had been invited as royal guest for that year. Her Royal Highness asked me how I felt to be beaten by my apprentice, to which I replied, 'I have to let him have his say occasionally!' As soon as the royal guest had left, a young lady standing in the crowd and whose name also happened to be Ann asked if she could purchase one of the pokers I had for sale. Later in the exhibition tent Brian enquired as to her opinion of the work entered for the competition. Unknowing who Brian happened to be, Ann stated that she preferred the entry that came second rather than the one that had been awarded first prize, only to be immediately taken aback by the young man's abrupt retort, 'The first prize is my piece!'

Brian became a highly skilled blacksmith, eventually gaining the Rural Development Association 'Apprentice of the Year Award.' He worked at Cupwood Forge for three years until starting his own business in a village some thirty miles distant. He had served us well, producing work of an excellent standard. Unfortunately he did not share my sense of humour, an attribute that few have managed to attain.

Catch!

On one occasion having driven to the local depot to collect two full cylinders of welding gas, I happened to notice the management had thrown out the showroom cylinders, which were made of fibre glass and had the exact appearance colour and size of their real life counterparts. These cylinders were so light that one could lift them with one hand. 'What are you doing with these?' I enquired, 'Scrapping them', answered the assistant. 'Can I have them?' I asked, 'Why?' he asked again, 'Cause

I can have some fun with these!' I replied. With my request granted I loaded them into the back of my pickup and returned to the outside of the forge, upon where I hollered, 'Brian!' Again I repeated even louder, 'Brian!!! I've hurt my back. Help me carry these cylinders in to the forge.' As Brian emerged from the door, I threw the oxygen bottle made of fibreglass in the air towards him with the cry of 'Catch!' His face immediately turned white and the cylinder being extremely light weight landed on the floor in front and bounced. Brian however failed to see the funny side exclaiming, 'I could have had a heart attack!' All said and done, I recollect that it happened to be me who could have suffered a heart attack from laughing!

Shortly after the County show, I met up with Ann again when demonstrating at our village fun day. It became the beginning of a relationship resulting in our marriage at Cupwood Church three years later. Brian had in the meantime married a local girl and invited us to his wedding, the reception being held in the function room of a local hotel. The meal followed by a disco turned out to be a pleasant and successful occasion though typical of many such events in this day and age. Such package weddings are extremely expensive and dare I say it? Bore me to death!! perhaps by that time Brian had forgiven Ann for her opinion regarding his winning entry at the county show. Ann had been divorced from her first marriage fourteen years before. She had two children John and Elizabeth, who have been constantly supportive throughout our life so far. Ann had solely brought her children up through financial hardship though still managed to continue her studies for an Open University degree in Art History.

Ann and myself began to plan our wedding differently, her side of the family had to journey many miles from the South Coast and I wished them to attend a totally unique enjoyable and memorable event that would be talked about in years to come.

The sun shone brightly as a 19th century landau driven by two dark bay horses, conveyed us the two and a half miles to Cupwood church and following the ceremony the horseman allowed the children of our guests to ride round Cupwood village. Forty-five guests attended a reception held in the village hall. The landlord of our local inn had prepared a magnificent buffet accompanied by generous glasses of champagne, wine and real ale. As our guests assembled I announced in a loud voice that everyone had to turn round and shake hands with the nearest individual. They were then, ordered to be seated next to that person for the meal, irrespective of which family they belonged. By making this happen, I had totally counteracted the tradition of having each of the two families sitting on separate tables.

At the appropriate time during the meal and true to my profession, I hastily donned my leather apron in order to cut the wedding cake with a hacksaw (clean of course!).

Entertainment followed the speeches and with two of my friends, we sang a selection of folksongs in close harmony much to the delight and applause of everyone present. Once the meal had ended and the tables and chairs cleared to the side, our traditional theme continued with further performances by a local group of Morris Dancers and folk singing by the 'Old English Pub Band'. Truly this had been a wedding to remember, one thoroughly enjoyed by all and at a fraction of the cost of if it had been held at the hotel.

Immediately after our wedding Ann and I spent our honeymoon touring the West Country, visiting the Cotswolds, the Forest of Dean, Bath and the Mendips, returning via the Wye Valley, Malvern Hills and Coventry Cathedral. Our trip unfortunately had coincided with an annual event in which I had taken part for the three previous years, demonstrating forgework at the American Community School, near Esher in Surrey, celebrating their 'Colonial Crafts day'. We decided not to let the school down, it had always been an enjoyable occasion especially as we were being paid for our services plus the travelling and accommodation incurred.

Unfortunately the only vehicle I had to transport the forge and anvil happened to be my open back pickup truck, hardly suitable for a honeymoon holiday tour, in fact the whole proposition of taking one's forge on honeymoon seemed bizarre in the extreme! The hiring of a small van for £60, seemed the ideal solution, at least the contents would remain invisible to the fellow clientele of the hotels in which we were to stay. Our demonstrations to the American children proved a success and the following day Ann and I travelled to the Cotswolds. Having stopped at some traffic lights on red, near Winchcombe, our van suffered the jolt of a car hitting us from behind. A lady driving her husband's Jaguar and failing to notice the lights being on red, had hit the rear of our van causing damage to the back door and bumper. I would imagine this would have been far worse had we not have been carrying a heavy anvil and forge in the back of the van. The damage to the front of the other vehicle happened to be far more serious as radiator, grille, nearside headlight and bonnet were in need of replacement.

The well dressed middle aged lady who emerged from the vehicle apologised profusely, asking that the repairs to my vehicle could be paid for by her giving me cash rather than going through her husband's insurance. I estimated it would cost in the region of sixty pounds to straighten the bumper and hammer out the dent in the door which she willingly paid.

I parked the van that afternoon in the corner of the hotel car park and with the manager's permission proceeded to use my tools and anvil in order to hammer out the dents and straighten the bumper. Other guests arriving looked in astonishment at the travelling blacksmith's show now set up in the car park of the hotel! A further two hours and my vehicle had been repaired, the dents had disappeared and the sixty pounds received would therefore pay for the hire of the van!!

Two days later I became engaged in conversation with the proprietor of a candle-maker's shop in the Forest of Dean, endeavouring to interest the fellow in commissioning decent hand forged candle holders to sell in his shop and also to display his work. Upon discovering the nature of my occupation, he asked if I would be prepared to make him a canopy and dog grate for the inglenook fireplace of his newly acquired farmhouse at the edge of a nearby village. I agreed to take on the commission and drove out to view the inglenook. It happened to be almost identical to the fireplace in Dr Broughton's lounge, which we had made as our first commission at Cupwood Forge.

Amazingly it had too been discovered upon the knocking out of a small Victorian fireplace which had been installed hiding the original hearth. The inside area of the inglenook measured twelve feet wide by six feet deep and incorporated stone bench seats at either end. The candle-maker related how one evening, immediately after moving in to the house, they heard footsteps walking up the stairs and across the upper floor. This became a regular occurrence and upon mentioning this one evening at the local village pub, the regulars commented that several previous owners had left after experiencing supernatural events in the house. In fact it had been rumoured for years that a body had been bricked up within the walls of the house.

Upon knocking out the Victorian hearth, a skeleton of a woman was indeed discovered laid upon the stone bench within the side wall of the inglenook fireplace! After a lengthy and fruitless police investigation to try and solve the mystery, the remains were buried in the local churchyard and the paranormal activity ceased. Six weeks later I returned to the farmhouse and fitted the canopy and dog grate, though I couldn't escape the feeling I was working in a mausoleum!

Our travelling blacksmith's show eventually became an established part of our business and way of life. In one particular year, I clocked up twenty-five venues, mostly in the South of England. In fact I had spent so much time away from the forge, certain customers within my home territory began to wonder if I had moved and discovering the forge closed, took their trade else where. As time progressed however, the increased cost of travelling encroached into our income and the profitability of our participation in so many distant venues therefore had to be questioned.

Even though the shows we attended had become an essential earner within our business, we had to learn how to sort out the best from the rest. The events that happened to be the most financially rewarding were based in the affluent South, the commuter belt of the metropolis. Had I not employed other trainees to produce the items for sale, I would not have found the time to attend the number of venues that we had booked. The show routine involved loading, half a ton of blacksmithing equipment, bags of coke and electrical gear into the back of my pick-up truck and always carefully packaging the ironwork that we had for sale. I have always sold smaller items such as candle-holders, fire-irons etc, that would require the minimum amount of space in the vehicle. Our small marquee including its framework required careful checking to make sure we had packaged all of our kit. In all, the preparation to attend a show took a full morning's work for two people and during the long journey that followed I always had the nagging worry of having left that all important item behind and incidentally frequently did!

By demonstrating the blacksmithing craft, it became obvious we were providing entertainment to the visitors of the show. It happened to be a service for which we frequently were paid and at the least being offered free trade stand space, which at events such as the Hampton Court International Flower show proved to be a magnificent opportunity. Our entertaining demonstrations were soon in great demand by craft show and event organizers, meaning that we could pick and choose as to which events we attended.

For several years we relentlessly journeyed many miles most weekends to venues in distant places though gradually however, we saw a decline in our sales and also the number of folk attending the shows. This deterioration seemed hardly noticeable at first, however as we compared figures and accounts with those of previous years the stark truth began to dawn, craft shows were failing, both in popularity and profitability. Today in retrospect, the reasons for this decline have now become apparent. In the 1990's a number of factors contributed to the decline in popularity of these events, to both the visitor and exhibitor.

1) The escalation of house prices and soaring mortgages meant that even the well salaried young professional couples had less spare cash in their pockets to spend upon hand-made items and luxury non-essential goods.

2) The so called 'global economy' has seen the demise of much of our manufacturing output and capability, high quality goods may now be imported from China and other countries and sold at little more than what we would pay for the materials.

3) As mentioned previously, the increased costs of motoring have also encroached into any profit that one is likely to make and combined with the high prices of accommodation and living away, the attending of events is an expensive affair. We always took our caravan to the distant shows we had booked, staying at approved touring sites that offered good washing facilities including showers. This proved extremely necessary as to the very nature of my occupation. Gradually we

upgraded our caravan, eventually being the proud owners of state of the art mobile accommodation, the purchase of which had required serious consideration.

4)   Finally the organisation of shows themselves has suffered due to the diminishing numbers of genuine craftspeople producing high quality hand-made products. Unlike craft shows as we knew them in the late eighties and early nineties, when many folk could virtually furnish their house from the quality craftsmanship on display, such events have now been largely replaced by marquees selling food, drink and fripperies.

It seems that in recent years the take up of exhibitors has gradually diminished and though craft shows still maintain a place in the public's day out calendar, it is no longer easy for organisers to populate their events with the number of genuine crafts people required. Many such shows are now having to resort to more entertainment in order to attract the necessary number of people through their gates.

5)   One important factor however, that has always determined the ultimate success or failure of any outdoor event, is of course the famous unpredictable, 'Great British Weather.' I have attended shows during which it has rained relentlessly from the moment the gates were opened to let the public enter the showground, to the moment that the Tannoy system announced the end of the event.

I particularly recollect one particular show held on a water-meadow and following a week of heavy rain the level of water in the river along side began to rise as we were leaving the ground at the end of the first days trading. Upon returning to the event the following day, an amazing sight revealed the whole area had flooded overnight to a height of two metres leaving only the tops of the tents and marquees visible above the newly formed lake. Many of the crafts people were in tears their whole stock had been lost, many not being insured for such a disaster. We however had fortunately set up our marquee upon some higher ground to one side of the field where the water level had only risen to a height below the tables upon which our iron-work was displayed. We were among the lucky few whose stock escaped, though later that morning, as the river levels subsided and along with many helping hands, I waded up to my waist helping other craftspeople retrieve that which was possible.

Iron in the Blood

Throughout the huge cross-section of society that visit and frequent craft and country shows, many individuals exemplify certain mannerisms and types. During numerous years of selling and demonstrating at these events, I have formed my own classification of the stereotypes that describe certain of the visitors and customers that have been to our stand. Please however don't form the opinion that every one of our customers are to be tarred with one of the brushes described below and we are grateful for the support of the many folk who have lovingly purchased items that we have made, I have however made certain light hearted observations of a few of the stereotypes who visit our stand.

Hardly a show goes by without Mr and Mrs Lovely admiring the ironwork on display:
'Come here darling look at these candle-holders, aren't they lovely!'
'Oh yes darling, they're absolutely wonderful.'

'Oh have you seen these fire irons they're lovely, if only we had a fire place they would look so lovely on the hearth!'

'And have you seen these wall oil lamps, what a pity we have so many pictures on our walls, otherwise we might have found just the place to display them, they're really lovely.'

'Well we've thoroughly enjoyed looking at your lovely display, we think you're a very clever man, making all those lovely items, we really do think they're lovely. Good bye.'

Mr and Mrs Hesitant would nervously approach the display and stand while staring in silence at the particular item in which they were interested. Minutes later one would speak; 'Is it a shade too tall darling?'

'It had crossed my mind, however it's certainly better that any we've seen so far,'

'Is it the right colour though? Will it match the pink wallpaper?

'Now that's a thought love, we'd have to really see it in position before we decide!'

'Mind you, we could take a chance and always paint it if it's not the right colour!'

'We could do that, but what if we ever get round to redecorating the room, it might look unsuitable for whatever makeover we give it!'

'That is a point, perhaps it would be better to wait awhile and think about it, sorry to waste your time young man, we may be back later!'

Mr and Mrs Haggle are frequent visitors to our stand; they study the work on display and converse in hushed whispers as if planning a campaign of attack.

'How much are those candleholders?' asks the wife, even though the prices are clearly marked.

'Fifty pounds each,' I would answer, 'It says so on the ticket.'

'How much would you charge if we bought three?'

Without smiling and fed up of selling, 'I'll sell you them for one hundred and forty pounds,'

'Would you take one hundred and twenty in cash?'

'One hundred and thirty five would be my final price'

'We only have a hundred and thirty pounds with us.'

'All right then, I'll wrap them up for you!'

Mr and Mrs Haggle would then move to purchase goods from the pottery stand next door, delighted they had made a bargain and try to repeat similar tactics with another craftsman all too eager to sell his wares at any cost.

Mr and Mrs Barter similarly would also try their hardest to obtain a bargain, even to the extent of no money changing hands:

'Grandfather died last year and left some old tools in the shed.'

'Yes I said at the time to keep hold of them as some one would be bound to have a use for them somewhere.'

'There's one of the funny vices similar to what you have, a box full of chisels and hammers and other old tools.'

'We don't live far away, would you consider a swap for some of those candle holders? 'I'm sure they'd be useful to you in your job!'

Mr and Mrs Nitpicker are the couple who find fault with everything; 'We are interested in your hanging basket brackets, however the paint on this one is missing at the tip of the scroll!' 'The left hand horn on this ram's head fire iron is a fraction lower that the right one! You have left hammer marks on the base of this candle holder and the right one is a touch lower than the left!'

'Considering these faults would you be prepared to give us a discount?'

Finally I must mention the names of two of the most frequent visitors to the show with whom we have to contend; Mr and Mrs Do you really make it yourself? and Mr and Mrs Three P's: Pick it up, Put it down and P**s off!

I have however, numerous fond recollections of the shows we attended and many humorous situations come to mind. For example, on one occasion, as we returned from demonstrating at a show in the London area, I drew up outside a corner shop to purchase a snack to fend away the pangs of hunger on the long trek back home. When the show had ended, I hurriedly loaded my stand, forge and anvil into the back of my pickup, hitched up the caravan and sped away in haste in order to make good time on the return journey. On leaving the shop I noticed a lady lifting a scrap cooker in to the back of my pickup, 'What on earth!' I exclaimed, 'You're the scrap wagon, aren't you?' enquired the woman,' it still works, I only want a fiver for it!' Shortly after my return home, I sold the cooker to a friend for ten pounds and as far as I know, it still works!

During one of my demonstrations at a venue in the vicinity of Gatwick, I attempted to complete another ram's head poker. Holding the item aloft in order to show it to the crowd of onlookers, I trod upon a tube of black grate polish that had fallen off the anvil and on to the floor. Immediately the black paste shot out of the tube in the direction of three young children observing me at work. Their clothes were covered and with serious consequences in the offing, my wife rushed the children to the first aid ambulance and began furiously cleaning their garments, completely exhausting their stock of 'mediwipes'. The treatment worked and the family, killing time at the show for two hours before flying off on holiday to Turkey, left with three children whose clothes were none the worse for the accident. The six year old girl however did not seem pleased, in spite of the fact that I had given each of the children one of our horseshoe puzzles priced at £10.50 to take away with them. 'I hated that Minnie Mouse T-shirt!' she said.

About half an hour after this incident had taken place, a young man in his early twenties asked if he could have a try on the forge. I replied that he would have to wear a spare leather apron and pair of safety glasses that I had brought with me. I carefully talked him through the making of a simple paper knife, in fact he found the experience so enjoyable that he asked if I would let himself and a friend come to our forge for a weekend to receive some more paid tuition in the subject. I agreed to this and arranged a convenient date. The day arrived and both men were given the task of making a hanging basket bracket and learning a great number of forge-work processes. Years later, when I had moved to Moslingham Forge and had three working forge hearths, I decided to repeat what then had been an extremely successful weekend, however this time teaching three students, one each per forge. I subsequently advertised these courses at the craft shows we attended and many would-be blacksmiths came to us for tuition. These courses also helped other establishments such as local accommodation providers and restaurants. Little did I realise what a difference these courses would make to our business in the future.

Gradually we became friendly with other crafts people who regularly attended the shows on our circuit, in fact a camaraderie developed among the group that pervaded the good and bad times we had together. At one particular event the organiser held a party on the Saturday evening for all the exhibitors. He provided a buffet meal and opened the bar for the

Harmonious Blacksmith

occasion. In order to provide entertainment he offered free drinks at the bar to anyone who would be willing to stand up and play, sing or tell jokes to the audience. In between my demonstrations that afternoon I began to paraphrase the words of the Major General's song from the 'Pirates of Penzance' by Gilbert and Sullivan; 'I am the very model of a Modern Major General'. That evening I nervously donned my leather apron and stood up in front of the audience and sang the following words:

I am the very model of a modern metal worker
1) I am the very model of a modern metal worker,
I hammer hard from dawn to dusk I can't be called a shirker,
I manufacture gates and grills, gazebos, garden furniture,
I am the very model of a modern metal worker.

Chorus;
He manufactures gates and grills, gazebos, garden furniture,
He is the very model of a modern metal worker.

2) I heat my iron in the fire to dazzling luminosity,
It alters all its properties to malleable plasticity,
My hardening and tempering gives tools their elasticity,
I've learned the very principles and practice of metallurgy.

Chorus;
His hardening and tempering gives tools their elasticity,
He's learned the very principles and practice of metallurgy

3) I demonstrate my craft at shows in any kind of area,
From stately homes to village greens to venues in suburbia,
I entertain the public with my skills and expertaria,
I am the very model of a modern metal worker.

Chorus;
He entertains the public with his skills and expertaria,
He is the very model of a modern metal worker.

4) Now my designs they are my own they really are superior,
I don't copy from catalogues; their work it is inferior,
I'm not a mere cold bender or a welder fabricator,

Iron in the Blood

I am the very model of a modern metal worker.

Chorus;
He's not a mere cold bender or a welder fabricator,
He is the very model of a modern metal worker.

5) I'm trained in business studies and the use of a computer.
Of cash flows, market forces and my economic future,
My V.A.T. is up to date, accounts are all in order,
For I am the very model of a modern metal worker!

Chorus;
His V.A.T. is up to date, accounts are all in order,
For he is the very model of a modern metal worker.

Chapter 6
The flames are quenched

Cupwood Forge became well known for its high standards of craftsmanship. Unfortunately we were severely restricted in our hours of operation, which in turn stifled the amount of work that we could turn out and therefore reduced our overall profitability. Our commissions were also increasing in size presenting ergonomic difficulties due to the limited space we had available in which to produce the goods.

Mr Grimbly took a week's holiday from work and spent time sorting out his garden, a piece of land overgrown and extremely neglected due to the two years that his house had remained empty. It became obvious however, that the sounds emanating from the forge were not to his liking and on one occasion he asked if we would refrain from hammering, as his young baby could not get to sleep. I replied that as the door of the forge had been closed, there happened to be little more I could do, as we had to complete the work in progress for delivery that evening. Mr Grimbly immediately threatened to report us to the authorities and obtain an order for the forge to be soundproofed.

The following week, a visitor to the forge introduced herself as the Environmental Health Officer for the district council and stated that further complaints had been received regarding noise pollution emanating from our premises. I became furious, asking the girl if the craft of blacksmithing should in her opinion be banned from villages where it has been practiced for centuries? I showed her the recent letter I had received from her department requesting we work according to certain hours, to which we had complied. I emphasised that Mr Grimbly had only complained after having been at home on holiday the previous week. Mr Grimbly, I stated knew he would be living next door to a working forge and therefore accepted his status quo. Finally I emphasised any closing down of the forge would result in the loss of a viable business in the community, including the addition of a further two men to the list of the unemployed! The Environmental Health Officer departed and no further letters were received.

Given a commission for a large quantity of railings, destined for a number of executive homes being built in a nearby village, we had to first complete the work that we had in hand. I had worked hard liaising with the builder and architect in order to gain what for us seemed a profitable undertaking. Houses were springing up fast in this location and therefore necessitated a quick sale. In retrospect, I should have been more realistic in promising the date of delivery however, restrictions in our working hours resulted in deadlines unable to be met. One morning the builder visited the forge, extremely angry that the commission had not been completed in the time stated, he gave us a two week deadline otherwise the order would be cancelled.

I had so far laid out a considerable amount of money in purchasing steel and materials, however I refused to be seen pleading with Mr Grimbly in order to gain the extra hours of workshop time required to finish the job. I therefore decided to enlist the assistance of another craftsman in metal, one who had helped us out on numerous occasions.

Bernie worked as a self-employed welder-fabricator, he appeared to be a no-nonsense individual of medium height, extremely short cropped hair and a neat triangular beard. He had the demeanor of an aged ex-boxer, who would still be able to floor any opponent in a street fight; his hard appearance however gave many folk a totally false impression, for underneath his rugged exterior lay a generosity which few would imagine.

He had a workshop that had once been a large brick granary barn, situated at the end of a long lane, in a remote portion of countryside, far removed from village habitation. The workshop contained a quantity of large sheet metal working machinery, a huge guillotine, hydraulic folder and a massive set of steel rolls; equipment that required space far in excess of the room available in our small village forge. Bernie had previously been the manager of a large sheet metal fabrication firm before its closure due to uneconomic viability at that time. He had purchased the equipment cheaply in the auction that followed and had also poached many of the firm's customers.

As I drove up to his workshop, Bernie happened to be opening the doors, having arrived just before us. I embarked from my vehicle and made to enter the building. Bernie immediately exclaimed in a loud voice; 'Don't move!' and ran to prevent me entering his workshop. 'Stay where you are!' he shouted into my ear! I happened to be petrified. What on earth could be the matter? 'Stay put!' he repeated and carefully disconnected a trip wire across the entrance.

In one corner of the workshop at waist height, a four foot square piece of heavy plate had been mounted on substantial brackets and fixed in position at an angle of forty five degrees. A sawn off double-barrelled shot gun pointed upwards to the underneath of the plate. Anyone unfortunate enough to activate the trip wire would have caused both barrels to spray shot at a height of three feet around the room. Bernie informed me that he had been broken into by thieves one evening and a large quantity of power tools had been stolen. A second time this happened however, after he had installed his deterrent, nothing had been taken though a small quantity of blood had been found on the floor. Bernie insisted that any wounds would not prove fatal, only painful. Needless to say he had never been broken into again.

On certain occasions Bernie had brought us work requiring such heat that could only be provided by means of a forge, however on our particular visit, I asked if he would help us assemble the railings so that we could meet our deadline and therefore keep the commission. Bernie agreed and for the following fortnight we worked at Bernie's workshop, from seven in the morning until eleven at night in order that the work would be delivered to the customer as promised.

The crunch of our dispute with Mr Grimbly came at eight pm one Friday evening, as I endeavoured to complete the painting of a pair of gates that had to be hung on site the following morning. I had heard my neighbour cutting his lawn with his new electric mower, creating a sound resembling the after burner of an air force jet taxiing along the runway. The sound ceased and half an hour later fuelled by a generous quantity of red wine, Mr Grimbly appeared from his dwelling motivated by a huge intake of 'Dutch courage'. Clinker ran to the closed double doors without barking, I knew that she recognised who happened to be the other side and therefore opened the door quickly.

Mr Grimbly who had been leaning upon the outside of the door with his ear firmly pressed to the woodwork stumbled in falling upon the floor. 'Good evening Mr Grimbly', I exclaimed, 'and how may I help you?' Our unannounced visitor stumbled to his feet and with a complexion resembling that of a jar of beetroot he shouted 'You've broken the agreement, I'll have you expelled from this place! Half past eight on a Friday evening and you're here making all this row!'

'Since when has a paintbrush made a noise?' I exclaimed. This now became the moment I retaliated, (verbally of course!) 'GET OUT!' I shouted, 'I'VE NOW HAD ENOUGH!' 'My business has suffered in trying my uttermost to placate your evil desires!' 'I've had enough I tell you!' 'This is now war!!' 'Just get out before I throw you out!!' Mr Grimbly then picked up an iron bar and went for me; we struggled and I threw him out of the door, slammed it shut and bolted the door from the inside.

Perspiration now dripped from my brow, I stamped upon the floor and proceeded to hit the hammer on the anvil as loud as I could for the space of twenty minutes. Again I stamped upon the floor and finally sat on the anvil with my heart thumping. I clenched my fists and nearly boiled over.

Rage gradually subsided and having made myself a cup of coffee, began to contemplate the way ahead, I had an idea and having found a blank piece of paper on my desk, wrote the following words:

The blacksmith worked at his anvil,
The village had need of his work,
From morning to dark, he hammered away

72

And never was known to shirk,
His contributions were many.
To farmer and villager alike,
He was willing to tackle any repairs,
From ploughs to mending ones bike.
For centuries his craft was vital,
To those who lived all around,
He seldom received any hassle,
Only admiration profound.

But gradually villages altered,
And houses were most desired
By city executives seeking recluse,
In a haven of fresh air and quiet.
The blacksmith was then viewed by many
As belonging to days long gone by,
The sound of his hammer and anvil,
Caused some to create hue and cry,
'We've come to this haven of quiet,
Not to be distressed by you,
Your grinding, hammering and welding,
Is a nuisance that never will do!

The village forge is now silent,
The blacksmith has packed up and gone.
No longer his fire is burning,
His anvil hammered upon.
The executive though still continues to moan,
Of noises and fracas around,
The clamour of cuckoos and combines.
Of cockerels and countryside sounds,
That disturb his haven of quiet,
His Sunday mornings in bed,
He still goes through life like a 'Wassack'!,
In spite that the forge is now dead!

The following day I posted my literary effort to the Standard, a local newspaper published every Wednesday. They duly printed the poem in their following issue. When at the end of that day Mr Grimbly stepped off the bus, carrying his copy of the paper under his arm, his face appeared as black as thunder, in fact I half expected lightning to strike from his nostrils. During the days that followed I had primed local people in the village to speak to Mr Grimbly, saying, 'Hello Mr Grimbly, we like the poem Fred's written about you!'

Mr Grimbly made an appointment in order to complain to Sir Walter, who exclaimed in his deep aristocratic voice, 'I knew Fred had established an excellent reputation as a blacksmith, however I take my hat off to his poetic skills! Frankly Mr Grimbly, Fred happened to be in the forge well before you arrived and is a useful craftsman to have in the community. If you're not happy I suggest you find accommodation elsewhere!'

Within a month, Mr Grimbly had moved to a neighbouring village and had rented a house next door to the village pub, which was a popular venue well known for its late night discos'. As far as I know he never dared complain regarding the noise from the village pub, even loud discos at twelve o' clock at night!

The village shop and post office also had a new tenant. Colin, a bachelor in his early thirties, who had been made redundant from a local engineering firm; one of many that had closed down due to the economic recession of the late eighties. Little was Colin to realise, that being able to run a small village shop as a successful business in such an economic climate, would only prove to be a pipe dream that would end in the same manner as the firm to which he had been previously employed.

Colin however epitomised the character acted by the late Ronnie Barker in 'Open all hours'. He wore a khaki warehouse coat covered in stains of all colours and twice a week he drove early in the morning to the wholesalers to replenish his wares. After six months, he only drove in once a week and the variety of choice for sale became noticeably less.

Unlike Mr Grimbly, Colin however, never complained about the noise from the forge, even though the buildings were connected. He remained a pragmatic though plausible character, extremely matter of fact and never without a smile, unfortunately jokes had to be explained, Colin would never recognise ambiguity and therefore became the ideal stool pigeon for an April Fools' prank.

And so whence opportunity presented, upon the first day of the fourth month, at nine thirty am, I gingerly opened the faded cream coloured door of the village shop. The door bell fixed to a spring mounting tinkled loudly, announcing my entry to the shopkeeper taking stock within the store room beyond.

Colin quickly appeared looking harassed and perplexed, 'Hello,' he greeted 'an what can I get ya?' 'Do you suffer from damp in your cottage?' I asked. Colin peered over his round thin gold rimmed spectacles as if I had verbally stirred the hornet's nest. He retorted that after relentlessly complaining to the Estate regarding excessive damp in the corner of his lounge, nothing had yet been done. 'The estate have just phoned through', I replied 'and at eleven o'clock this morning, they have arranged for a guy with a dampometer to measure the moisture content of your walls'. 'About time!' Colin exclaimed, 'now at last something may happen and I can get round to decorating the room, a job that should have been done months ago!' 'That's not all,' I stated. 'The Estate has requested that you thoroughly soak the outside walls of your house to a height of six feet, approximately one hour before the fellow appears.' Colin's face changed to bright red, his eyes protruded from their sockets behind his glasses and resembling an angry crustacean, he bellowed, 'WHAT ON EARTH! I'm on with my stocktaking today, how on earth am I to do that?' 'Use either buckets of water or a hose-pipe,' I replied, trying to grit my teeth in order to keep a straight face. 'Ah well, if it means that my damp problem will finally be cured,' he retorted, 'I suppose I'd better get on with it, the hose-pipe will do the job quicker!'

Shortly after, Colin appeared with a hose-pipe, directing the jet of water upon the front of the house without realising that he had left the front window open. He dropped the pipe and rushed into the dwelling to close the sash window that had jammed within its frame. After tugging violently for a full five minutes the window closed and Colin returned to continue the task of hydrating his home. A group of villagers were walking down the road and on seeing Colin's aquatic antics, crossed over to the other side in fear of being soaked themselves. We've heard about car washing!' they shouted, 'didn't realise your house was that dirty!' Colin continued undeterred, regardless of the growing crowd of onlookers that had gathered at some distance in order to behold the curious spectacle. 'Need any shampoo?' one humorous villager enquired. Eventually Colin became satisfied that the walls were well wet and made to turn off the tap. 'Colin,' I shouted, 'What day is it?' Colin turned round and without realising replied, 'April the First'. The crowd of onlookers collapsed in hysterics and Colin shouted, 'You B_ST_RD!!'

An agricultural engineer, working in much larger premises in the next village, had decided to vacate the building in order to work from his own property, a small farmhouse some three miles distant. I immediately applied to Cupwood Estate for a transfer and moved in soon after the property became vacant.

The premises consisted of a large seventeenth century granary barn containing a brick forge hearth that had been built at one end. A small door at the opposite end led to a cattle shed with a hay loft directly above. The high roof of the building contained many large timbered beams giving the premises a unique old world character. At a much later date the building had been enlarged by means of a workshop in the form of a brick built lean-to, which extended along its full length.

Moving from a tiny village forge to such vast premises presented a formidable challenge as my apprentice Brian had moved on to further his career, leaving me to soldier on regardless. I had thought long and hard regarding the move, especially as to whether I would be able to meet the financial commitments required. The very nature of our craft, with its high skill content, necessitates serious training; it is not learned quickly and upon being approached with an offer of a business partnership, by a blacksmith who had recently moved in to the area, I accepted, though not without reservations.

Richard had previously worked for a large firm of architectural metalworkers in Peterborough, he proved to be an exceptional welder though his forgework skills required improvement. We were, in the beginning, fortunate in gaining some large commissions and these gave us the incentive to work together. My stepson John left school at this time and joined the team as a trainee.

Ann had by now obtained the position of Exhibitions Organiser for a gallery in the city, its purpose was to give young artists their initial opportunity to hold an exhibition of their work. Each chosen artist would receive a grant from the area arts organisation of two hundred pounds to fund publicity for the exhibition and its setting up expenses, including wine and invitations for the preview. On one occasion an artist had unfortunately dropped out and at short notice Ann had been left with a vacant space in her calendar. Ann asked me if I would be willing to create an exhibition and fill the gallery with contemporary ironwork, however I had only three weeks in which to get my act together.

In the meantime, I had to convince the trustees of the gallery that I was capable of producing an acceptable display. The interviewing panel were extremely sceptical arguing their whole philosophy would be destroyed if work contrary to their aims were exhibited, i.e. principally fine art and sculpture. The trustees allowed me, by a narrow vote, to go ahead. Members of the committee were worried as to how a village blacksmith, who in their opinion allegedly repaired plough shares, could be capable of producing innovative art work of a contemporary nature.

My business partner Richard did not however agree to this opportunity saying, 'How on earth could we speculate on three weeks work being recuperated with hard cash in the hand?' In spite of his complete lack of faith, I decided to proceed. I had a vision, an opportunity, which could make or break my career. Unequivocally and taking the bull by the horns, I decided to 'go for it!' Fired up and brimmed with adrenaline and enthusiasm, I spent an hour sketching my first design, a four foot high sculpture of a ballerina forged from a single length of six inch by half inch flat section steel bar. The work took two days to produce in fact I nearly gave up attempting acrobatic techniques under our newly acquired power hammer. The finished piece finally held all the qualities of its intended subject, exhibiting graceful movement and flow, I now had sixteen days left and had to fill the gallery.

The days crept by and being enthused with a psychological high that I had previously rarely experienced, my adrenaline sustained my efforts from seven in the morning until eleven at night. Even then I still found time to sketch out my next piece of work. Eventually the time arrived when our work had to be arranged in the gallery.

The catalogue of my work included:

Four foot high forged ballerina,

Contemporary fire dogs and grate for eight foot long fire place,

Contemporary garden gate,

Pair of two foot high contemporary candleholders,

Four foot square contemporary window grill,

Three foot high electric wall lamp forged and textured from six, inch by one inch steel strip,

Pair of small candle holders,

Contemporary table lamp and bowl,

Free standing forged flame sculpture five foot high,

Poker brush and shovel, each three foot long,

Vase of flowers,

Massive sculpture of two hand forged swans and signets,

Contemporary forge hanging basket bracket,

Fruit bowl (1),

Fruit bowl (2),

Organic sculpture from tube,

Contemporary three set square plant stand.

The moment came when the gallery doors opened to reveal the preview of my first solo exhibition entitled, 'IMPACT'. During the previous three weeks, as I relentlessly toiled, forging through my designs, I considered frequent headlines for the posters that would advertise the display. The chosen caption said it all, 'The impact of the hammer upon the white-hot steel and the visual impact of the resultant artwork to the observer.'

Contemporary art previews have become a unique institution, comprising an unequivocal and motley collection of society, its devotees being

Dancing in Iron

drawn from the academia, affluence and individuals with creative and sometimes pretentious aspirations.

First to arrive at my preview were two artist friends of mine who worked in jewellery and ceramics. I had met them at local craft shows many years earlier. Although their financial situation probably restricted their purchasing power, I valued their opinions and constructive criticism as they had participated in many exhibitions themselves. Pam and her partner, Tony were also excellent folk musicians who frequently performed at various venues in the county. Both had a typical hippie appearance; Tony's face happened to be mostly obscured by a huge brown beard, he had long hair down to his shoulders and wore a huge multi coloured sweater, knitted with a bold zigzag pattern. Pam sported a long wool dress adorned with many long strings of heavy beads that complemented her partner's identity. They stayed for the majority of the evening, mingling with the powers that be and with every intention of promoting their own business and situation.

Following hard on their heels were Margo and Bertie, both of whom were regular devotees of major art exhibitions in the city. Margo a late middle aged lady always wore smart colourful expensive and fashionable dress that complemented her slim figure. In spite of her increasing years, Margo captivated group conversation, though as the evening wore on, aided by numerous glasses of wine, her speech became increasingly slurred. Margo had acquired property and money both through legacy and the divorce from her first husband, a wealthy solicitor who had exchanged her for a younger model many years before. Her present partner Bertie, a tall, slim, bespectacled guy wearing a pink bow tie always seemed to walk behind Margo in a supportive and subservient fashion, his smiling face epitomised an aura of utopia especially when his wine glass had been refilled. The pair lived in a large Victorian house furnished with nouveau works of arts and crafts that over the years had virtually become a gallery in its own right. They have purchased a number of my works and I am grateful for their support.

Margo and Bertie had met up that evening with Jan and Eddie, an extraordinary couple who had moved from London three years previous. Eddie had been fortunate in selling his property in the south at a premium price, therefore creating a substantial nest egg to live a comfortable life in our part of the country. He enjoyed the social intercourse of the preview, being a cheerful cockney character. Recognisable by his short cropped hair and large saucer shaped ears that protruded from each side of his round jovial face, I jokingly remarked that he resembled a thatched cottage with its front and back doors open. Eddy's partner Jan wore a long silk dress in oriental style with floral design, her waist length jet black hair gave her a far eastern appearance. Unfortunately Eddy's appreciation of art extended no further than page three of the tabloid press, his loud comments were on many occasions an acute embarrassment to those standing nearby. I have grave doubts whether their house contained any art work, as I had never seen them purchase any item from the previews they attended.

Within half an hour of opening, the gallery was full; the area Arts Officer, gallery trustees and various associates were huddled together in one corner, earnestly engaged in conversation. It soon became apparent however, they were not in the least interested in the work I had made. Upon pointing this out to a friend, he replied: 'Not to worry as the so called arts establishment only came to these events out of duty, as being part of their work.' 'They attended so many previews, that any novelty factor had long since disappeared, exhibitions no longer held any interest for them!'

The showing of my work however, happened to be a great success. I had excellent write-ups in the local papers, comments in the visitor's book were amazing and best of all nearly every piece had been sold including a candle holder which to my surprise had been purchased by Eddy and Jan!

Some weeks later, I received an invitation to attend the preview of an exhibition of bronze sculptures by an up and coming female artist, who had been given an Arts Council grant in order to travel to Alaska for inspiration and ideas. On the evening of the event, Ann and I travelled to the venue, held at a well known gallery in the city and having suitably parked our vehicle arrived a couple of minutes before the exhibition opened. Posters advertising the exhibition were displayed on the gallery's glass door, I became intrigued to read the details about the items on display entitled; 'Piss Sculptures in the Snow'.

The doors were eventually opened to reveal a large spacious room containing a number of small white plinths, each approximately two foot square and one foot high. Upon these stands were mounted the upturned cast bronze sculptures, also painted white; they appeared to resemble small fairyland castles, as if made from melted toffee poured from a great height and although similar in appearance, each had its own peculiar composition of many stalagmital shapes. The scene appeared surreal; bemused visitors to the preview carefully stepped around the many ethereal polymorphs gazing in bewilderment, one could actually sense a united lack of comprehension and understanding.

Slurred Speech

Risking the catching of severe exposure from the extreme subzero Alaskan night, our intrepid artist had ventured outside, squatted down and urinated in the snow, wiggling her rear at the same time. The following day she poured synthetic resin into the cavities produced by the hot liquid as the surrounding snow had quickly frozen solid. When set, she removed the resin which eventually became the patterns from which the bronze casts were made.

About ten minutes after entering the building, in breezed Margo and Bertie making a beeline for the wine table, having already consumed a quantity of liquid in various localities that afternoon. Neither appeared to notice the work on display, Margo's conversation however seemed preoccupied with the eloquence of adversity. Obviously fuelled by alcohol, trivia had turned to turmoil, their speech sounded exceedingly slurred, which gave me an idea. I hurriedly made my way to write my comment regarding the exhibition in the visitor's book and found to my delight that no one else had yet written theirs. This brand new hard backed manuscript had been provided especially for this particular exhibition, to which I wrote in large letters on the first page the immortal words:
'AT LAST A REAL PISS ARTIST!!'.

As the evening progressed I took delight in the observation of visitors writing their comments in the book, all happened to look over the previous comments, facial expressions ranged from outright laughter, disguised sniggers, puritanical stares to horrific bewilderment.

Today art can mean all things to all people, its evolution during the past century has gained such a momentum that in some aspects it is difficult if not impossible for the ordinary man in the street to understand. Logical comprehension seems to have disappeared clean out of the window. Contemporary art appears to be no longer concerned with the management of the visual but rather the employment of conceptual surprise intended to shock and bewilder. Some of the winning entries for the 'Turner Prize' are prime examples.

This present philosophy of art is now and sadly, perpetuated in our leading art colleges and universities. What initially began with the employment of lateral thinking has now progressed to a sad situation where the blind are leading the blind rather than opening ones eyes to an appreciation of aesthetics and form. I have however no intention of misleading you into assuming that I only appreciate photographic realism such as the precise fine art paintings and sculptures that try to be accurate visual depiction of the subject. My objection lies when art resorts to gimmickry as a means of creating a pseudo elitism of intellectual pretence and thereby manipulating a grossly inflated market for a worthless product!

My own attempt to employ genuine lateral thinking at a local art exhibition turned sour. The event held annually in a local town hall attracted many folk who came to purchase paintings of idyllic country cottages, seaside images and country landscapes as well as local crafts, such as wood turning and pottery. I had been invited to exhibit my ironwork and came up with an idea that might create some controversy, whilst at the same time depict the quality of our work and design. I manufactured three wooden plinths approximately 3ft square and 2ft high. Upon each one I placed a pile of off-cuts of steel bar, short ends that had been left over from the manufacture of a gate, a balustrade and a garden seat respectively. I electric welded the off-cuts together in the position they assumed upon being tipped into their heap so that they could not be taken apart. The three plinths and their contents were placed along side the gallery wall allowing me to display upon the wall above each plinth a large photograph of the finished gate, balustrade and seat. I assumed that visitors to the exhibition would relate each pile of off-cuts as an aesthetic by-product of each of the finished pieces. I named each mound of scrap: Gate, Balustrade and Garden Seat accordingly and waited with apprehension and bated breath for the reaction of the punters.

Very few of the viewing public however seemed to understand the association between the photographs and the mounds of scrap steel, 'How on earth could this be a gate or that a garden seat?' were the comments. The local press published angry letters from various members of the public who thought I had lost the plot and accused me of trying to undermine their intelligence with such a time-wasting exercise. Needless to say I have never been invited back to that venue again.

This experience taught me a lesson, even though I had genuine avant-garde intentions, they were not to be imposed upon those whom art meant solely, visual enjoyment and photo realism. Perhaps an exhibition at some appropriate venue frequented by those appreciative of modern art would have provided the stage for my lateral and diverse concept, who knows?

Public art can also be even more controversial as it is on view to everyone, not just those who frequent galleries and exhibitions. We have been involved in many public art projects in our career, mostly with appreciative acclimation. There are always however, those with whom art belongs to page three of the tabloid press and state that the cost of art in public spaces would have been better spent upon street lighting, car parking and improved litter collection. Personally however, we have managed to produce certain styles of work that move the boundaries of our craft forward in a positive direction, whilst at the same time proving to be attractive and saleable pieces of work to a contemporary market.

My artistic aspirations only contributed to conflict within the firm and it soon became obvious however that the partnership was doomed to failure. Richard did not share my enthusiasm for forge-work especially artistic and sculptural. We frequently argued and after nearly three years in working at Lower Britwood, John and I left the forge, moving to the blacksmith's shop at Moslingham that had once been the workshop owned by the late blacksmith Percy Joyston, whose famous hammer had been lain to rest in the museum as previously described.

Chapter 7
The flames rekindled

The solicitor's draft of the partnership dissolution stated that I had not to work a forge within a radius of twenty five miles from Lower Britwood. Moslingham was a small village thirty-five miles distant. My wife however had no intention of moving home and therefore every working day for the following eleven years, John and I journeyed a seventy mile round trip to work and back. The journey through beautiful countryside had a therapeutic and relaxing effect, the roads were mainly quiet and uncongested though the occasional hazard of ice and fog required extreme care when driving.

Our first day at Moslingham Forge had necessitated driving through snow and ice. We had been given the key from our Landlord some two weeks before, however Christmas had intervened and now duly refreshed from the winter break, John and I opened the double doors and stepped into a blacksmith's shop that had been locked and bolted for ten years..

After the death of Percy Joyston, a local business man had bought the forge for his son in order to start a career in blacksmithing. Unfortunately the lad had met a fatal accident whilst motor cycling at a local racing circuit. The forge had then remained an unopened shrine to their son until his parents decided to lease the workshop to a successor.

Setting off from home on the 2nd of January, a white carpet of snow melted slowly as we drove carefully along the country roads aware that other vehicles seemingly oblivious to the hazards ahead overtook at speeds that far exceeded consideration of safety and common sense.

The early morning sun, a massive bright fireball emerged above the horizon shining directly in our direction, therefore creating a further hazard in negotiating our drive to Moslingham. Throughout the eleven years that followed we gradually became acquainted and familiar with its spectacular scenery, changing seasons, variations of weather conditions and alternatives of route. The majority of the time we travelled feeling calm and relaxed, even though sometimes, difficult moments and schedules of work lay ahead. I doubt if life would have been the same if we had to experience an odyssey through traffic jams, lights at red and the urban congestion experienced by many town and city commuters who arrive at work thoroughly stressed and bothered.

Excited and apprehensive, I turned the rusty old key stiffly within the lock, allowing the bib and brace door of Moslingham Forge to creak open revealing a scene reminiscent of years gone by. Ancient tools, agricultural implements, artefacts littered the floor, benches, shelves and tool racks. The bright light of the sun shone through the window illuminating an incandescent canopy of cobwebs whose trapped insects created weird and eerie shadows upon the opposite wall. The building reminded me to some extent of Ben's workshop where I began my career as a smith and incidentally images from my childhood as I peered through a murky window in order to watch the blacksmith at work.

I realised a huge task lay ahead, and once again, I happened to be only answerable to myself. My imagination brought me back in time. I was ten years old again, however this time I happened to be in charge.

The forge and its shoeing area were confined to one room, approximately twenty foot wide and twenty five foot long. It contained two brick forge hearths, each with the traditional twisted chimney. An original 'Blacker type' electric driven mechanical power hammer stood within the small space between. The anvils were placed upon tree stumps extremely low to the ground, this seemed to explain why my memories of the old incumbent Percy Joyston, were of an elderly bespectacled man having the stature of a gothic arch. His acute stoop happened to be the result of many years hammering upon these low anvils. I have no intention to end my years in a similar manner and consequently work upon an anvil placed higher from the floor. It has to be realised however that a heavy blow exerts more force when the hammer strikes the iron at a lower position due to a maximum delivery of swing. This in turn means that work can be forged and drawn down more quickly.

As one faced the forge from the road outside, the property appeared to consist of a motley collection of low buildings each in different style attached to each other. An open timber-framed storage shed some twelve feet wide and twenty feet deep joined the left hand side of the forge and had been a storage area for lengths of iron and steel bar. Two narrow low pantiled brick buildings were attached to the right hand side. These had once been a primitive cottage Percy however, had used them as a store room and hardware shop selling general ironmongery to the local community. These buildings were full of a variety of boxes of nuts and bolts, screws and hinges. Percy also had sold paraffin, stored in twenty gallon drums which were housed within these buildings. Piles of harrow teeth and farm implements were stacked virtually to the ceiling and crude hanging basket brackets, weather vanes and fire-irons were displayed for sale.

I now regret having not taken any photographs of the forge at that time as they would have made an important contribution to any local historical publication.

Within two hours of entering the premises I had a fire blazing away in the forge hearth, though it took four weeks of hard work before we had the workshop in some semblance of order. Gradually the forge took shape to our liking, the end room became a gallery and show room, the middle room a layout area and welding enclosure and a third forge hearth became added to the main area creating a facility in order to teach the craft however on a small scale.

The majority of our old customers found where we were now working and contacted us for more work. I explained to them how Richard still ran the forge at Lower Britwood and they could have taken their trade to him, many however stated that I had been the blacksmith they had dealt with in the past and that it was their prerogative to trade with whom they chose. Word had also reached the Local Town Council that blacksmiths had moved into Moslingham Forge.

The historic Regency Town Hall of Busford was currently in the process of a major restoration and a new mahogany handrail had been made to replace the original that had decayed over the years. The removal of this rail from the heavily ornate cast iron balcony had caused many breaks in the cast iron to spring apart and therefore weaken the structure. These breaks had to be welded in situ. The contractors however had been told that the use of naked flames during the restoration was prohibited in all circumstances due to the tinder dry wooden floors and fabric. After much consideration and debate the council reluctantly agreed for us to weld on site provided we employed the necessary fire watch and screening.

John and I complete with three fire watchers armed with a multitude of extinguishers began the cast iron welding of hundreds of breaks in the balustrade. The pure nickel cast iron rods were extremely expensive the breaks had to be ground into grooves in order to fill with the weld. The work took two weeks to complete and without a hitch so far we had reached the final two feet of balustrade adjacent to the magnificent pipe organ for which the building was renowned. As the very last break was being welded we noticed a wisp of smoke emanating from a mouse hole in the floor boards at the side of the organ. The smoke stopped and everyone breathed a sigh of relief, however two minutes later a large amount of smoke began pouring out of the hole. Visions of the Town Hall burning down sprung to mind, the ensuing consequences and the embarrassment that would destroy a promising career. In an instant we emptied a whole co2 fire extinguisher into the hole with a force that would exterminate resident rodents within a radius of 20ft. However unknown to ourselves, underneath the balcony, perched upon the top of a ladder, happened to be a painter placing the finishing touches of gold leaf on the plastered cornice. The craftsman stood relaxed and content, proudly surveying his handiwork when without warning the full force of high pressure co2 shot out of a crack in the ceiling and into his ear. Our friend managed to hold on to the ladder thinking his time had duly come at last. Many of a weaker disposition would have required psychiatric counselling and incidentally that also nearly applied to ourselves.

They say everything happens in three's, and following in quick succession came two other jobs involving electric welding within the confines of tinder dry and historical properties. A telephone call from a local builder invited us to price up some work at Godesley Hall, a 17th century country residence built for a former Lord Mayor of London at that time. In recent times the building had remained in an empty neglected condition following its previous use as a psychiatric rehabilitation institution. The new owner had built houses upon the lands of the estate and had decided to convert the Hall into a residence for himself and his family.

Godesley Hall, built on the brow of an escarpment, happened to be a beautiful period house with terraced gardens overlooking a lake. Our client wished to convert the cellars into a large area in order to garage his vehicles. Automatic shutter doors had been installed in a completely new entrance to this area intended to be accessed from the lower left hand side of the building. The original wooden ground floors of the house were now required to serve a dual purpose and become the ceiling of the garage area. They were tinder dry and required support using large steel joists that had been placed in position with the verticals supporting the horizontal steel beams. This underground area now resembled one level of a multi-storey municipal car park however these fourteen inch steel beams required welding together in close proximity to the lath and timber ceiling. Again I had visions of the historic building on fire and the ensuing consequences; did I happen to be out of my mind even to contemplate such a task? The steel beams required a heavy duty weld for adequate penetration of the joints this required a large current and much heat.

After much thought I agreed to do the work providing: 1) The client insured the work himself, 2) He had a team of fire-watchers armed with extinguishers above and below the ceiling, continuing their watch for a full twelve hours after the welding had all been completed. 3) That he employed two plasterers in order to cover any exposed timbers with wet plaster in and around the vicinity of our welding. It took two days of careful work to complete the task without a huge conflagration at Godesley Hall,

Our third example of what could have been referred to as 'pyrotechnic madness' came about when we were asked to build a massive safe for a wealthy client within his large country manor house. This safe, the size of a small room, had to be manufactured from steel plate and covered on the outside with firebricks. A massive security door resembling the entrance to a bank vault had been purchased in order to be attached to the front of the steel box.

The project required much welding, again in close proximity to the tinder dry fabric of the building. The safe door weighing approximately one ton, had to be carefully lowered into position on the lounge floor using a forklift truck poking its tines through the open French window doors and moving to position at the front of the safe by rolling on short lengths of steel tubing. We had provisionally welded a primitive steel jib to the steel casing above the frame of the safe door; a chain hoist attached to this jib lifted the safe door into position. Our safe was finally welded together from the inside after being covered with fire bricks and the strong room, when completed, had to be camouflaged by a false wall acting as a secret door that opened electronically. Much thought and planning was undertaken before the work commenced, I had dreaded thoughts that if the structure had not been constructed completely level, the safe door would swing to by means of gravity and trap anyone unfortunate enough to be inside. When the moment eventually came to test whether or not this would happen, the client appeared for the first time and much to our relief our project was demonstrated to be a success.

Having just returned from demonstrating at a craft fair in the South of England I answered the telephone, not realising we were about to embark upon one of the strangest commissions to date. 'Am I speaking to the blacksmith?' the voice enquired. 'That's me.' I replied cheerfully. 'Do you manufacture garden pot holders?' he continued. My initial thoughts were of small brackets or stands produced in large quantities for garden centres or private clients. I therefore cordially agreed to pay the prospective client a visit, totally unprepared for what lay ahead.

A couple of days later, I navigated the narrow country roads, arriving mid morning at the client's house. Judging by the huge expanse of a massive yew hedge surrounding the perimeter of the property, I suspected the house itself would be equally a grand affair. However due to the sheet metal backdrop of a large pair of wrought iron entrance gates, it happened to be impossible for me to see what lay beyond.

Nervously I pressed the keypad to announce my arrival, a metallic voice replied through the intercom, enquiring as to who had arrived? 'Blacksmith,' I stated and with a whirling sound the gates slowly opened to reveal an extremely long driveway, bordered again by two tall yew hedges. It was only when I arrived at the end of the drive that I had my first glimpse of a large modern executive dwelling, built in Spanish style, overlooking a large heated outdoor swimming pool.

The house however didn't happen to be what immediately caught my attention; upon the lawn and lying upon their side were two of the largest terracotta vessels I had ever seen. Each pot eighteen feet from end to end had a curved profile tapering to a point at their base and obviously Mediterranean in style. I began to wonder how on earth these vessels would function as being unable to stand vertically in position.

Our client, a small stocky man in his fifties, came to the door and over a cup of coffee explained that he imported 'Amphora'. These were earthenware vessels used in the Mediterranean countries to keep commodities such as wine, grain etc cool by placing the pot in the ground with the neck at floor level. He continued to explain that these, as far as he knew, were among the largest pots ever to have been made. They each took a year to build by means of a coil technique and fired by building a charcoal furnace around the outside of the vessel, enclosed by means of an outside wall made from clay. The charcoal would then be lit in order to bake the pot.

Our client had been offered a prime position in the centre avenue of the Chelsea Flower Show at the last minute due to a space being made vacant. He required the manufacture of two decorative steel stands in order to hold these vessels vertically and asked if we would we be able to achieve the work within three weeks? As usual, I couldn't resist a challenge and agreed to the commission. The proposed stands had to be attractive in design and appearance, a circular ring with three vertical legs would not be in order. I therefore began sketching a number of designs. Each vessel weighed two tons and would not be placed into their holders until two days before the show opened, when a specially hired crane would lift them into position.

My chosen design, forged from four inch by one inch section steel under the power hammer gradually took shape. One particular problem had presented as how to take an accurate measurement of the curvature of the side of each pot. I made a huge try-square out of square tubular section. Placing one side across the top of the vessel, I carefully took measurements from the adjacent side at four inch intervals to the outside curved edge. We were then able to plot this curve in chalk upon the concrete floor of the assembly room back at the forge.

Each assembled stand weighed approximately one ton; they took the weight of their pot down through a shape similar to the base of the Eiffel tower. The finished and painted stands were loaded by forklift onto a lorry and taken to the show; they looked aesthetically pleasing however, I did not know for certain that they would hold their pot without undue movement or collapse.

On the day prior to the show I received a phone call informing that the lift had been a success and virtually no movement had occurred. These huge amphora became the talking point of the show, The then Prime Minister and Royalty gazed aghast and marvelled at these gigantic exhibits, another achievement for the forge!

The Blacksmiths' Association had accepted an invitation to take part in a 'Blacksmithing Extravaganza' in Southern Ireland and organised a coach for members willing to attend the event and to continue their journey from the ferry across the Irish Sea. We had only to pay for our bed and breakfast accommodation, our travel and food being paid for by grant aided funding from various sources in Ireland. The programme of events constituted a welcome barbecue meal on the first evening sponsored by Guinness. News that one could help themselves to a free bar sped throughout the local community, who quickly availed themselves of the facility, needless to say the barrels soon ran dry and everyone retired to their digs happy though thoroughly tired after an extremely long journey.

The following day dawned and after breakfast the blacksmiths met in the market square where a number of forges and blacksmithing equipment had been assembled. The plan of action was to make a sculpture for the town comprising a collection of individual designs produced by the various smiths and welded together into one piece. I had an idea and forged the Guinness harp, the piece happened to be appreciated by all and I became known as the 'Harp Smith',

A Ceramic Challenge

Unfortunately principles of health and safety were decidedly lacking in those days, electric welding for example being carried out in full view of the general public. I remember one fellow shout, 'Com here Shamus! com and look at da bright loit.' I'm sure many folk must have been affected the next day by sore eyes and arc-eye!

93

Iron in the Blood

Shortly after, I was approached by the organisers of a famous craft market that held a massive folk and craft event over the May Bank Holiday weekend; they wished to make blacksmithing the focus for this event and asked if I knew any other blacksmiths who would demonstrate their work. I had an idea and wondered if I could organise an event similar to the one we had attended in Ireland. Consultation began with the craft market committee, the district and town councils, arts associations, sponsors for steel, coke, transport of equipment, marquee hire, publicity and the many other items that constitute the organisation of a major event.

The day finally arrived, bringing forty blacksmiths from Britain, Ireland, and France. The weekend commenced with a trip round the steelworks before arriving where the event was to be held. The Town's Chamber of Trade had organised a welcome buffet meal with big band entertainment at the local Grammar School.

Fourteen forges had been assembled close to the craft market in a roped off area and next day the hearths were lit as we commenced to produce a large decorative archway and two side panels containing individual designs to the theme of heritage and folk.

The work, completed in time, is now recognised as part of the County's Arts Trail and is a lasting momento of when the blacksmiths came to town. John and I finished, painted and sited the archway. The event, though extremely successful, had nearly burnt me out and I now had to return to the everyday routine of earning a living; the days leading up to this event had resulted in such work being neglected.

Chapter 8
Distant fires

Having been threatened with dire consequences if I did not take a holiday, I decided that we would take the caravan and have a break touring North Devon and Cornwall. Ann particularly enjoyed this part of the country and as I had never visited the area before was quite happy to let her organise the route, the places to visit and stay. Our small caravan had been bought second hand from an elderly couple who had placed an advertisement in our local paper. It happened to be a 'Van Royce', well known for its quality workmanship and design. Ann decided that we should break the long journey down to Woolacombe by having an overnight stop at a small Caravan Club site at the village of Stortsbury in Wiltshire. The village fortunately had a fish and chip shop and therefore we were able to eat a hearty meal without having to prepare one ourselves. Later, I took the dog for a walk and having attached her lead to one of the wooden benches in the beer garden of the Blacksmiths Arms, I duly walked inside to order a pint of their Best Bitter.

The village inn and its thatched roof had a great character, one could have stepped into a time capsule. I doubt whether the walls, tables and benches had been replaced for at least two hundred years. In keeping with its name, various blacksmith's tools and artefacts were displayed around the room. I began to wonder if I could really escape from the craft after all! The beer and cider were poured directly from oak barrels resting upon trestles behind the bar and being a fine sunny summers evening, I took my pint outside, finally sitting on a bench, relaxing and watching the fast flowing ripples of the stream flowing through the bottom of the garden. The Landlord came into the garden collecting the empty glasses that customers had left upon the tables. 'Noice evenin,' he said. The landlord, a tall distinguished man in his early fifties, had a large head of thick greyish black curly hair, circular thin rimmed spectacles and a greyish black beard. 'An arr ya on olidey?' he asked in a broad West Country dialect. 'Heading there,' I replied, 'but having a stop over at the caravan site in the village as we're driving down to Devon.' We continued talking for quite some time and after discovering that blacksmithing happened to be my occupation, he bought me another pint and asked if I would make him a large log rake and poker for the old inglenook fireplace in the lounge of the inn.

The following day we journeyed on through the Mendip Hills, stopping at various places of interest, including the Cheddar Gorge and Wookey Hole. That evening, as we arrived at the caravan site at Woolacombe, we were welcomed by one of the most glorious sunsets I have ever seen. Having once sited our home on wheels, we could do nothing else but stare westwards out to sea, mesmerised by the changing colours, until the last vestiges of deep purple hues were snuffed into oblivion.

As the week progressed, we continued to explore more of the coast, eventually reaching Tintagel. No sooner had we paid a small fortune for being able to park our vehicle in the town, the skies darkened and rain began to fall with increasing ferocity until a downpour of immense magnitude turned the streets into rivers and their gullies into rapids. As did many other tourists, we fled, taking cover inside the local church until the storm abated some thirty minutes later. Emerging from the building we gazed in amazement at the flooded gardens, alleyways and roads.

Tintagel and its so called association with King Arthur and the Knights of the Round Table attracts tourists in their hundreds of thousands. Arthur, according to tradition, had been a 5th century warlord who fought against the Saxons. His story gradually became embellished with the many anachronistic attributes that have established the now well known saga of King Arthur and the Knights of the Round Table. Arthur and his association with Merlin, Sir Galahad, Camelot and Tintagel, all help to make good reading promoting the numerous sales of souvenirs and making excellent business for the many gift shops in the town.

Personally I have no objection to the combination of Legend and Tourism, however by the time we left I felt over indulged, having completely had my fill of false frippery and foolish fantasy!

I often wonder how many of the thousands of holiday makers who flock to the area arrive with sincere intentions of appreciating the beautiful coast, its scenery and areas of solitude and isolation? Most however seem to gravitate to the main coastal resorts such as Ilfracombe and Woolacombe, sitting in deckchairs huddled together on a crowded beach eating candy floss and fish n chips.

A few miles along the coast, we headed down an exceptionally steep and windy road to a small inlet and sandy cove sheltered by an ampitheatre of rugged towering cliffs. A small flat lay-by provided the perfect space for parking the vehicle which we temporarily abandoned and made our way to the water's edge. It seemed we had arrived at paradise, beautiful warm sunshine, a placid calm blue sea, golden sands and our only neighbours being the watchful sea gulls oscillating in the rising currents of warm air, gliding backwards and forwards and occasionally coming to rest upon a rocky ledge high above.

Our holiday couldn't pass by without the exploration of parts of Exmoor, the geological guardian of the South West Peninsular with its bleak summits, steep valleys, fast flowing streams and small villages nestling within its rolling foothills. From the coast some miles away, we could discern the heights of the moor land plateau covered with a topping of early morning mist that shimmered in the rising sun as if being a distant lake in a far off land.

The steep windy narrow roads and high hedges were certainly not built to accommodate large vehicles and high speed traffic. I apprehensively approached each bend wondering if the vehicle that we were about to meet travelling in the opposite direction had the same concerns and caution as ourselves. On one occasion, as we entered a small village, with its quaint cob houses, I could not help but notice a familiar long low, outbuilding, recognisable by its wide open double doors, single chimney, and racks of rusty iron bars outside. We parked on the roadside and entered the forge in order to introduce ourselves to the blacksmith inside. He happened to be a member of the Blacksmiths' Association whom I had met at a conference three years earlier. Roger made us a mug of tea as we earnestly began to talk shop, Ann by this time had begun to assume our so called holiday was turning into a blacksmiths' convention and though accepted her drink, politely intimated that unless we quickly made a move she would catch the next bus back to the caravan site.

Hardly had we begun to relax and enjoy our holiday than the time came round for us to prepare for the long drive home and on this occasion we would not be having an overnight stay in order to break the journey. The owner of the caravan site had entrusted me with two antique iron entrance lamps for complete restoration. The origin of the lamps was unknown however they seemed to have had a nautical origin as if having been designed to illuminate the bow of an ancient sailing vessel. Each lamp stood five foot tall, they were six sided and consisted of a robust forged wrought iron frame in order to hold the glass. The ironwork, including the curved hexagonal tops, was made using traditional techniques including tenon joints and rivets, therefore giving an indication of age and value. Although having been converted to electricity, I became convinced the lamps had been originally illuminated by oil or gas. They were extremely heavy and had suffered acute corrosion from the salty sea air over many years.

The owner of the site obviously had to be sure that he had entrusted his valuable antique lamps to a genuine craftsman and not to someone who would keep them for his own intentions. I showed him my portfolio of work and he also phoned one of our regular customers as a reference. I immediately booked another week long stay at the caravan site in the forthcoming Autumn, when we would return with the fully restored lamps; to our delight the owner promised us a free stay when we returned.

The week had literally flown by and I had quickly come to the conclusion that we had hardly scraped the surface, discovering the mystery and magic of this wonderful part of the country. However the time had come for us to hit the road and begin our long journey home.

Our vehicle left the holiday site at precisely 7.30 am, towing a caravan grossly weighted down with the huge iron lamps that we had placed inside. I realised however, we would have to drive carefully and not to speed over uneven surfaces approaching corners and bends with extreme care. Two miles down the road I stopped at a filling station for fuel and the checking of our tyre pressures. Our return journey now commenced with earnest determination, I required all the energy and concentration that I could muster.

Having taken the shortest route possible to the motorway, we were seemingly making good time when I noticed a blue flashing light in the mirror of the vehicle. Carefully I manoeuvred and stopped on the hard shoulder, I ventured outside to meet the two policemen who had flashed us down.

Almost immediately a second patrol vehicle drove up and then another. By this time I began to think we were in serious breach of the law and visions of another type of holiday were running through my mind. Suddenly three of the police officers were scrupulously checking the vehicle, its tyres, and worst of all, attempting to peer inside the caravan.

The first police officer spoke, 'Are you the owner of this vehicle Sir?' 'Yes officer,' I replied nervously as it seemed that we had become the focus of a large police investigation. By now the number of flashing lights had grown to such proportions as to represent a major motorway incident and curious passing motorists were slowing down, therefore causing a huge tailback of traffic.

'May I see your documents?' asked the policeman. Fortunately I had brought photocopies of my insurance, driving licence and vehicle registration with me in case of such eventualities. 'These are photocopies, not the originals,' exclaimed the officer, 'I need the originals for verification! Could we have a look inside your caravan please?' I opened the door and two officers stepped inside and after a few moments came out carrying one of the iron lamps. 'Where did these come from?' one enquired.

By now I felt helpless, how on earth was I to convince the police that all happened to be perfectly legal and above board. 'Have you radioed your headquarters and checked the ownership of our vehicle?' The police officer confirmed that he had already performed that task when following us before stopping. I now resorted to another line of defence, showing him one of our business cards from out of my wallet and also my portfolio of work in order to prove the nature of my occupation and business. I related how we specialised in the restoration of period and historical ironwork. I gave him the phone number of our client at the caravan site in order that he could verify the truth of our statement.

Fortunately the Police Officer accepted our explanation; however he expressed concern as to how the rear of the caravan had been observed to be extremely low to the ground. Requesting therefore that we redistribute the weight over the axle and drive more slowly, he explained how many architectural antiques were being stolen from large houses and gardens by travellers in order to sell at antique and collectors events and therefore he had to be sure that we were legit. The officer also requested one of our cards in the event he ever required any quality ironwork to be made for his house.

The incident had delayed our journey for about three quarters of an hour. I then decided that it would be better if we broke the journey, staying at another caravan site in order to complete our journey home the following day. I have always considered that the purpose of a holiday surely is to help one relax and to return calm, invigorated, energised and refreshed having fully charged ones batteries in order to cope with all future obligations and opportunities. I have seen so many return from holiday thoroughly stressed after driving exceedingly long distances and looking far worse than before they began their long awaited break!

We left the motorway, its crowding and congestion south of Evesham, making our way to a small Caravan Club site situated in a small village at the edge of the Cotswold Hills. Having sited the caravan and removed the lamps safely to the vehicle, we walked along the road in order to have a meal at the local inn.

The tranquil village of Brinscombe and its picturesque buildings were indeed the perfect ending to what had been a memorable holiday. The village inn, renowned for its excellent and yet inexpensive cuisine, added that extra charm and unexpectedly concluded a holiday well deserved. We arrived home at three-o' clock the following afternoon ready and prepared for any onslaught that may follow!

Chapter 9
Fiery Storms

Moslingham became hard work. I endeavoured to visit prospective clients in the evening or on Sundays, leaving me as much time as possible during the week to forge and manufacture our orders and commissions. Pressure presented itself in many guises, working all hours began to tell, local work was only to be had if our firm could compete in price with the fabricators and cold benders who produced cheap decorative ironwork at little more than the cost of the materials. Frequently I travelled many miles, spending huge amounts of time in order to design and quote for ironwork that ultimately was given to other manufacturers. Perhaps my enthusiasm for the blacksmiths' craft blinked the profit that could be produced from work of a lesser quality. The reality is that the majority of the public cannot tell the difference between hand-forged scrolls with traditional tapered ends and those where the steel is bent cold around pieces of steel tube.

To those uninitiated and uneducated in our craft, all decorative ironwork is visually a combination of curls and bends however well produced. I have known many a blacksmith producing high quality ironwork trying to compete in price with Joe Bloggs and his electric welder manufacturing a sub quality item in a fraction of the time.

The education of clients in order that they may appreciate and pay accordingly for the quality of craftsmanship offered is an extremely difficult exercise of diplomacy and persuasion.

Our work frequently became the relentless toil of the treadmill of turnover, working all hours in order to keep the Bank Manager, the Taxman and the VAT Inspector at bay. Somewhere out there must be clients who would appreciate our work and pay accordingly!

A public art commission came to our rescue; for once we were paid a realistic design fee and a decent hourly rate for a number of community workshops, producing ideas which were to be incorporated in the final work. No sooner had we completed this work than another pubic art opportunity came our way. I realised that this ought to be the direction we should take and having subscribed to a national periodical that advertised commissions specifically for artists, I religiously studied in detail any opportunity that seemed suitable. Once again however, I fell into the rut of tedious applications. Each issue of the magazine contained no more that twelve suitable advertised commissions and considering the sheer number of applications received for each, the chances of being invited for interview became a remote possibility.

Applying for such commissions became an expensive undertaking, digital cameras were at that time still in their infancy and all such applications required the inclusion of a number of 35mm slides or transparencies of previous work undertaken. Certain commissioning bodies also required preliminary designs being produced for inclusion with the application and determined artists would therefore spend hours of unpaid work for submission only to learn that their work had been refused without the decency of explanation.

Many city, district and county councils employ a Public Arts Officer whose responsibility involves the commissioning of art in public spaces and throughout our career, we have been fortunate enough to have taken part in such projects. Arts Officers come and go and frequently having built up a good relationship and reputation with one person, we find that we have to begin all over again when dealing with their successor. Many Arts Officers refer the task of awarding work to private commissioning bodies. These are often distant organisations which have no understanding of the proposed situation of the work, the area, geography and social history. I distinctly remember pubic art being commissioned for three towns in our County and not one local artist even being given the opportunity to submit a proposal for the work.

One morning and feeling distinctly unwell, I asked John to travel to Moslingham by himself. At 7.30 with our dog Clinker riding in the passenger seat, he set off for the forge driving our blue Toyota pickup truck. I had been suffering sickness throughout the night and had remarked that if I felt better later that day, I would make my way to work in my own vehicle.

The morning sun had already melted away the misty beginnings, promising the warm and glorious day that beckoned. Only upon extremely rare occasions had I spent time away from work due to feeling unwell. I've known those who use any excuse to have time off work, though when self employed, the situation is different, there is no one to offer sick pay, it's simply a work or lose situation!

Half an hour after John had left, our telephone rang; it happened to be a Sister from the County Hospital saying that our son John had been involved in a serious road accident and had been airlifted to hospital by ambucopter. He had suffered a head-on collision with a large water tanker. Clinker had been killed instantly and my stepson had suffered severe injuries.

Hurriedly Ann and I quickly packed John's pyjamas and toiletries into a holdall and sped off to the hospital.

John was not a pretty sight, almost every bone in is face had been broken, together with his right arm. Although still extremely dazed, he recognised his visitors and uttered the words, 'Sorry!' We realised that he had been extremely fortunate to survive and that rehabilitation would be a long process. We stayed the night in one of the bedrooms which the hospital allocated to surgeons on call. The doctors had decided to send John down for surgery that evening, the first of a number of delicate operations required in order to rebuild the bone structure of his face. I had virtually no sleep and when morning dawned, we hurried back to the ward to be with our lad when he regained consciousness from the effects of the anaesthetic.

At three o' clock that afternoon, we journeyed a further twenty miles from the hospital to collect what personal items could be salvaged from the wrecked vehicle, including the shattered remains of Clinker. The

Toyota pickup that John had been driving was unrecognisable, being now a mangled twisted concertina of scrap steel. How on earth the boy had escaped alive seemed a miracle beyond comprehension, driving home I uttered a prayer of thanks. Someone somewhere had been his guardian angel. We had collected Clinker and brought her back home to rest in our garden; she had reached the grand old age of fourteen, having lived a happy and carefree life. She had entertained all and sundry, a canine character and now hopefully chasing beer mats in that grand kennel in the sky!

Slowly, painfully and with great determination John travelled through the long route of recovery, though I now had to bear the brunt of performing the work of two men. I worked extremely long hours, manufacturing during the day, visiting clients and producing any necessary designs in the evening. The long arduous days began to tell, tiredness developed slowly and unnoticed into lethargy and mental confusion. I began to make mistakes and eventually realised that if I continued down this road, a nervous breakdown would soon enter the equation. One hundred percent work and no relaxation is a recipe for disaster.

I had previously taken on work for two men and now our impatient customers were beginning to hassle; fortunately a few realised our predicament and sympathetically were prepared to wait accordingly. The very nature of our craft requires years of training and experience and those who have worked towards this are mostly self employed within the confines of their own forge. Where on earth was I to find a replacement of the calibre and training of John?

Desperate for another architectural blacksmith to work with us at Moslingham, I began to draft an advertisement that I could place in the local press and the employment agency. No sooner had I put pen to paper than the telephone rang, it seemed an answer to prayer, a miraculous solution to our problem. 'Is that Fred Pope?' enquired a voice in a distinct West Midlands accent. 'I've just moved into the area with my new wife,' he continued 'and recently left the army, where I was a blacksmith in the Royal Electrical and Mechanical Engineers, REME for short.' 'I can forge and weld and am looking for work as a blacksmith.' I agreed to meet the applicant in order to discover more and arranged an interview the following evening at our local pub.

Steve happened to be living in rented accommodation not far from our village, a tall and stocky character, he seemed an honest and plausible fellow. Steve told how he had recently relocated from Hampshire in order to avoid trouble from his wife's ex husband and having retired from the services now required civilian work. He also related how he served as an active member of the Royal Antideluvian Order of Buffaloes, a secret society similar to that of the Freemasons devoted to charitable works.

I agreed to give Steve a fortnight's trial to test his application and skill, little was I to realise what lay ahead! Steve related that his father had recently retired from blacksmithing and shortly would be visiting him at his new home. After his fortnight's trial I agreed to employ Steve, though unknowingly, this was to become one of the greatest mistakes I have ever made.

Steve's knowledge of blacksmithing happened to be of a basic level, he showed however a reasonable proficiency in electric welding and fabrication. Together we managed to reduce the backlog of work and four months after his accident, John resumed his work, though without necessary hindsight I mistakenly made the decision to continue employing Steve. My first indication of instability within the status quo happened to be upon returning to the forge one morning after visiting a client in a neighbouring village. As I left my vehicle I heard loud words and shouting emanating from inside the building. Upon entering I heard the words, 'How you can show your F'n ugly face in public without making everyone sick, I don't know.' 'Don't ever look in the mirror you'll scare yourself to death.' 'What the hell's going off?' I exclaimed. 'Oh, I'm just telling him how the army treats its wounded,' he replied, 'it's their way of instilling confidence in their soldiers.' 'If I ever hear anything like that again,' I said, 'you and me will part company for good!'

Steve journeyed to the forge in an elderly Ford Corsair, he also drove a brand new state of the art BMW high performance motor cycle. It became some surprise however when one particular morning Steve asked if he could borrow one of our two pickup trucks, as the engine of his car had ceased to function. 'What is wrong with travelling to work on the bike?' I asked, 'It's not always easy,' he replied 'especially when the weather is bad!' Out of kindness I temporarily loaned him the vehicle we had recently bought to replace the Toyota destroyed by the accident, another huge mistake that we were soon to regret!

During the few weeks that followed, many unfortunate occurrences happened; individually they seemed innocuous, however when later viewed collectively, a sinister picture emerged. Power tools such as angle grinders suddenly ceased working, important hand tools essential to everyday working in the forge could not be found; the main bronze bearings of the power hammer developed such an extraordinary amount of play that effective working became impossible.

Upon driving back from hanging a gate at a nearby village, I hurried into the forge to answer the phone that I heard ringing from the office. Later, upon arriving home, I opened the glove compartment of the vehicle in order to retrieve my invoice book, which I had placed inside on leaving my last customer. The invoice book containing the record of four months invoices was missing. I diligently searched the vehicle only to no avail. A sleepless night ensued. The following day was spent in retracing every movement of the previous day. I turned the office inside out clutching the straws of remote possibility, hoping that I had inadvertently misplaced the missing article in some obscure location. My wife advertised that the book was missing on the local radio. Upon remarking to Steve that my last resort would be to report the matter to the police, the book mysteriously reappeared under the driver's seat of the vehicle, a location I knew had been searched a few days previously.

Some weeks later, Steve failed to report for work and never came back to Moslingham Forge. We shortly heard from one of our trading Reps that he had set up his own business and had rented a small forge some forty miles away. Curiously our Rep remarked that although Steve had not yet set up an account with his firm and neither purchased any consumables, he had noticed that upon the shelves on the end wall were boxes of grinding discs, rotary wire brushes and many other consumables bearing the trademark of his firm.

It became obvious that during the time Steve had been working for us he had gradually filched these items with the sole intent of setting up his forge with a large amount of the consumables and tools necessary to kick-start his new business into operation. Furthermore he had written to many of our past customers saying he had previously worked for Moslingham Forge and had now set up by himself producing work to our standard at a cheaper rate. Steve could not have acquired this information without access to our invoice book, which incidentally would have given him the information necessary in order to price his work.

Some weeks later, I began to notice a knocking sound emanating from the engine of the vehicle that had been loaned to Steve and progressively getting worse during the days that followed. Eventually the vehicle began to loose power, diagnosis revealed that the big end bearing shells had worn down and the engine required replacing at a cost of £2000. Weeks later, in conversation with another local blacksmith, who had been visited by Steve, I learned the rogue had boasted how he had placed valve grinding paste into the engine oil of the vehicle and also in the lubricating grease that we regularly applied to the bearings of the power hammer. It was then that I decided to relate what I knew to the police.

The officer from the C.I.D. doubted whether we would be able to prove criminal misconduct in court, I therefore suggested that the police at least perform a check to find out if Steve had any previous criminal record and gave them Steve's national insurance number.

The more I thought about the situation, the more I became convinced that Steve must have previously had a chequered history. Why had he suddenly escaped from his home in the south to begin a new life in our neck of the woods? Behaviour such as this can't happen all of a sudden, a leopard cannot suddenly change his spots!

A few days after my visit to the police, Steve suddenly upped and went. His neighbours related how at two in the morning with few belongings, Steve, his partner and her five young children left the house in his dilapidated pickup never to return, the almost new BMW motor cycle being abandoned for the council to collect.

Blacksmithing is a craft where its practitioners generally help each other. I have known numerous occasions when a craftsman has farmed work out to others due to him being busy with other projects at the time. If Steve had been genuine he would have informed us of his decision to set up on his own, it did not occur to the fellow that we would have helped him to do this and probably have offloaded him with work when we were extremely busy. Blacksmithing is also a small world; our association is such that any person like Steve would soon be known where ever he decides to roost. I have made many enquires however and to my knowledge Steve has never in this country, resurfaced again as a blacksmith.

Years later however and on one particular occasion when I happened to be teaching a short course in blacksmithing to a small group of students, I was informed of an Englishman who had moved to Spain, visiting blacksmiths there in order to find work. The student who mentioned this had himself moved from England to live in Spain some eight years before and had set up his forge in the outbuildings of his country house. He had paid for tuition at our forge in order to learn more advanced forgework techniques. Our student related how on one occasion a stocky guy with a Birmingham accent arrived at his forge, enquiring about the possibility of obtaining some work. He introduced himself as Phil and described how he and his family were now living in Spain after moving from the UK six months previously. Fortunately our student informed the guy that he could under no circumstance find enough work to offer employment to anyone at that time.

The situation now could only improve. John had made a good recovery and our reputation for quality work was spreading far and wide with many commissions emanating from the craft shows that I attended and demonstrated at on a regular basis.

One morning a young lass visited the forge, enquiring if we would provide two weeks of work experience as part of her 3D degree course in metal design at university. Helen, a slim, petite, extremely attractive girl with long blonde hair, appeared to be the antithesis of what one would expect of any one associated with blacksmithing, indeed her appearance would more likely have led one to believe that modelling or fashion had been her chosen career. Her timing could not have been more fortunate, as it so happened that we had been given a small public art commission to produce contemporary railings around a 'Heritage Room', located within a small country village in the south of the county. The commission involved design workshops working with the children at the local primary school. I asked Helen if she would care to organise this project and arrive at final design.

Having seen the sheer fluidity of our style of forge-work inspired by organic and natural shapes, Helen decided to ask the children to create flowers in modelling clay. These could then be created in steel as railing terminations. We have frequently used this material in our design process. I have often stated that shapes produced in modelling clay can be replicated in hot iron.

Helen had a natural gift in working with children; the flowers they produced were amazing, many of the designs were copies of existing flowers such as tulips and daffodils, however a few of the pupils exercised lateral thinking in order to create flowers of their own design. One young wit for example modelled the shape of a brain surrounded by petals and exclaimed that he had designed a brainy flower. Forging the designs were fun, Helen proved that the task of wielding a hammer didn't present a problem in fact she skilfully executed many of the designs before leaving to return to university at the end of the fortnight she had spent with us.

We invited Helen to attend the opening ceremony at the village when the railings had finally been painted green and erected on site. The pupils, under the supervision of their Head Teacher, had then to paint at a later stage the flowers in bright natural colours using enamel paints of their choice. During the unveiling ceremony the chairman of the school governors officially accepted the railings and gate on behalf of the village. The immaculately dressed and well spoken lady, who also served as chair of the Parish Council and as an elected District Councillor, stated how she preferred the railings in their existing plain green colour and apparently for reasons unknown, her word happened to be the final say in the matter. I became incensed; it seemed as if half the project had been axed by a self opinionated dictator and for someone, especially in her role as chairman of the Governors, to deny the school children the experience of adding colour to their creations seemed disgraceful. Wouldn't it have been a dreary world if all its flowers had been created green?!

I remember the day Helen arrived at the forge to inform us that she had graduated with honours. I had been so impressed by her contribution to the flower railing project that we offered her employment at Moslingham Forge, especially producing the smaller items which were displayed for sale at the country and craft shows we attended.

For the time being work happened to be in plentiful supply, our reputation for craftsmanship and quality spread far and wide, especially through being noticed at the craft venues that we attended. Our phone never seemed to stop ringing, in fact I jokingly threatened to have the phone company investigate my forge hearth as every time I placed a piece of iron in the fire the telephone seemed to ring!

On one occasion I answered an enquiry from Gordon Barnes, the head of house at one of the countries largest stately homes. 'Would we be interested in providing a quotation for the restoration of historical and prestigious iron railings that were attached to the stone dwarf wall overlooking the terraced rose gardens of the house?' Endeavouring to reply in as professional a manner as possible, I asked if we could arrange a site visit in order to assess the condition of decay and estimate the required work and the cost involved.

The following Sunday afternoon, Ann and I approached Brocklesford Abbey for a meeting with both Gordon and the Duchess herself. The midday sun shone as a golden orb illuminating the stately scene as the large Elizabethan house appeared as a prominent feature in the landscape. The house, village and estate lay among the beautiful valley of the River Dawn encompassed by distant limestone hills and moorland plateau's capped with glistening purple heather. Stationary white plumes of cloud stood as guardian sentinels above the horizon, otherwise the clear blue sky enhanced the sheer beauty of the scene. Gordon had requested that I phone him to announce our arrival at the gate and our mile long drive flanked by an avenue of majestic limes seemed in some sense almost supernatural as a stroboscopic sortie of sunshine and shadows swiftly ushered us along.

Immediately having entered the paved courtyard and parking our vehicle in front of one of the many coaching stables, Gordon emerged from a side entrance of the house in order to escort us to the large patio overlooking the terraced gardens. The Duchess opened one of the French windows and walked out to join us, enquiring if we would enjoy a cup of tea after our long journey? Our meeting lasted about one hour, during which I made a detailed assessment of the work required. This would be our most prestigious project so far, I estimated that the project would take at least four months to complete. I journeyed back home excited and elated.

Although I had to provide an official written quote, Gordon had intimated that my verbal estimate would be affordable, providing we would be able to begin the work immediately in order to finish before the start of tourist season when the house and grounds would be open to the public.

I now realised that in order to address this commission with all due justice it deserved, I had to offload the other impending work, which I gave to two other reliable blacksmiths in the area. The initial preparation, site-work and logistics, had to be planned out meticulously; the removal of the ironwork from the stone housing in order to be cleaned accordingly and the employment of a stone mason in order to make professional repairs to the stone walls. A considerable amount of time had been spent initially in the office organising the impending work and shortly before we were due to begin disaster struck with vengeance

They say everything happens in three's: Firstly John's accident, the sabotage and havoc reaped by Steve and now 'Foot and Mouth'! Upon replacing the telephone handset after receiving the news that the railing restoration project had been postponed indefinitely due to the closure of the estate, I felt gutted. Dazed and stunned in disbelief, I sat at my desk staring into thin air and even more bad news had yet to come; nearly all our country and craft shows had been cancelled because of the precautions that had been put in place due to the outbreak of the disease.

With virtually no work on the books I lay in bed that night trying to contemplate the way forward, somehow I could not sleep, we had already suffered financially from the mischief and mayhem that Steve had reaped upon us. Our overdraft had been high and I seriously expected the bank to foreclose, wages and suppliers had to be paid, our transport costs were high, the taxman also required his bite of the cherry, a fruit which did not seem to exist.

I discovered shortly afterwards that the banks had a graded list of trades and occupations that assisted them when deciding whom they would be willing to help in times of hardship and difficulty. Unfortunately blacksmithing did not rate highly on this scale and therefore a short time later I happened to be summoned for an interview with our Bank Manager in order to be informed the bank would be reducing our overdraft facility by stages throughout the coming months.

Thoroughly disillusioned, I drove to work as if the world were about to end. Has all my hard work over the years been in vain? The bank had also refused to pay a couple of cheques including our rent and had imposed severe financial penalties that only resulted in our overdraft increasing accordingly.

Trapped within the treadmill of unremitting toil I soldiered on, grasping at any straw that came my way; small jobs often at prices little more than the cost of the materials, solely in order to maintain some semblance of cash flow. Profit seemed an illusion, a mirage that in reality could never be attained, and many other similar businesses seemed to be in the same boat.

An enquiry from the local district council asking if I could manufacture the framework to hold interpretation signage seemed promising; these steel frames were intended to house the art-work and text describing to tourists information relating to particular places of interest. I had to quote for the manufacture, painting and siting of the frames and also the employing of an artist to paint the necessary work. I thought long and hard as to how we would approach this commission. How much would a professional artist charge for painting up to a maximum of ten images on a board complete with all the necessary text?

Glancing down the workshop and seeing Helen hammering away on the anvil, I had a brilliant idea. 'Helen.' I called. 'Could I have a word?' Seeming glad of a brief respite from hammering away Helen sat down in the office. 'You studied Art,' I remarked,' Were you any good at painting pictures?' Helen smiled and replied, 'landscape and figurative painting have always been one of my good subjects.' I informed her about the possible commission and suggested using a computer to achieve the signage. Some time previous I had purchased a second hand computer of limited memory, plus monitor and printer to use purely as a word processor for typing letters. My idea, if feasible would be to upgrade the computer and purchase a scanner and digital camera. From digital images of the content required for the information boards, we would have watercolour paintings produced, which in turn could be scanned and manipulated on the computer. A professional printing firm would receive the artwork on disc in order to produce the final result, an ultra-violet resistant print that could be placed beneath a clear polycarbonate window within the galvanised and painted steel frame.

Helen agreed and after our quotation had been accepted by the Council, I managed to scrape up the necessary in order to purchase the computer and necessary equipment. I now had to learn the photographic and drawing programmes required, not an easy task for an amateur, however eventually and with the help of others more accomplished in computer graphics I achieved a reasonable level of competence at the task. Our first board happened to be the local Town guide that had to be situated in the market square. Helen's paintings were of an excellent standard. At long last it seemed as if light had appeared at the end of the tunnel.

The local District Council commissioned a total of twelve individual interpretation boards, though six of the locations required a duplicate board placed at some distant position. The work had to be completed within a specified time due to it being grant aided by European funding and this meant that Helen and I had to work extremely hard in order to deliver the goods on time. Fortunately we were supplied the necessary text and details of images that were required by the council. I certainly learned a huge amount of local history and knowledge within a short period of time. My acquisition of I.T. and computer skills proved invaluable for other projects that followed; our bank balance now seemed much healthier and furthermore I felt a much happier person.

Other major commissions followed in quick succession, one being the design and manufacture of contemporary railings, door handles and altar furniture for a brand new church and community centre, built to replace the original that had been destroyed by fire two years previously. We were now in the fortunate position of employing another apprentice to help cope with our increasing workload.

Another project involved working with a firm of historical cabinet makers to reproduce the ironwork required for the oak travelling furniture of King Henry VIII. The commission involved working to detailed drawings and specifications researched by an archaeologist employed by English Heritage.

During the three months that followed, a total of twelve chests and eight packing cases were manufactured together with four thousand hand-made nails and a multitude of hinges, hasps and lock plates. They included a reproduction of the King's huge treasury chest, completely covered by overlapping bands of iron for security purposes.

We breathed a huge sigh of relief when having finally completed the work in time for the opening of the exhibition at Dover Castle. English Heritage seemed delighted with the furniture we had produced; the frequent visits to our forge by the archaeologist ensured that a high standard of craftsmanship had been maintained. Our cabinet makers and the archaeologist were however horrified to learn that another firm who had been commissioned to manufacture reproduction Tudor tables and furniture had used veneered MDF in its construction. This seemed an insult to all our efforts in ensuring that traditional materials and craftsmanship had been so faithfully observed in the manufacture of our work.

Chapter 10
Avenues of flame

The heat became almost overpowering as I increased the flow of propane supplying our new large gas forge, reported to be the mother of all gas furnaces. The ordinary coal or coke fire can only accommodate two or three pieces of work at any one time without one or more melting in the heat, hence the saying: 'Too many irons in the fire'. Many other colloquialisms which we use in our every day conversation originated in the village smithy, sayings such as: 'Strike when the iron is hot', 'When I nod my head, hit it!', 'Getting hot under the collar', 'Nose to the grindstone', 'Losing ones temper', 'To strike a deal' or 'Forge a bargain'. The auctioneer's hammer is also a symbol of this tradition.

The gas forge however can heat and hold a large number of items without them overheating and although it will not achieve the high melting and fire-welding temperatures of the coke forge, it is ideally suited to high volume production work at a maximum of 1300 degrees C.

On this particular occasion I had to re-forge, grind, harden and temper 300 jack-hammer points and chisels for a local tool hire firm. These are the tool bits that are used to break up concrete and stone. The steel we use is extremely tough and even though I was fortunate to have been using a power hammer, they had to be finished off by hand.

Steel contains a mixture of the metal iron and a small amount of the chemical carbon. When the carbon content in steel exceeds 0.8% the steel can be made hard by cooling quickly in water or oil. When this has happened the steel is also brittle due to carbon atoms being trapped within the molecular structure. By heating this steel to around 350 degrees centigrade, a number of carbon atoms are freed and the steel can lose a certain amount of its brittleness, yet retaining the majority of its hardness; this process is called tempering.

In the forge we use the 'one heat method of hardening and tempering', whereby the cutting edge end of the chisel is firstly heated to red heat for a length of approximately six inches and cooled for approximately three inches in water or oil upwards from the tip. We would then quickly hold the chisel in the vice and use a portable angle grinder to both clean and sharpen the tip. Due to part of the chisel still being at red, the heat gradually travels down towards the tip. We can observe the oxide colours forming as the freshly ground steel eventually oxidises to purple. When this has happened the tip of the steel is quickly dipped again in water cooling and drawing out the remaining heat and giving the tool its correct properties in order to perform its intended task.

On many occasions we had large quantities of points and chisels to make good for use. The gas forge would enable up to six tools at a time to be heated and remain at bright red heat without fear of burning in the fire. One had to remember however, that steel kept in a gas forge for too long a period would become severely oxidised and covered in a thick layer of scale.

The re-forging of jackhammer points and chisels provided, at one time, my main source of income though it soon became apparent that fumes from constantly quenching in oil were having a detrimental effect on my health. I had increasingly developed a smoker's cough even though the operation was being carried out in a well ventilated space. At one time we sharpened the tools for nearly all the plant and tool hire firms for miles around, however our turnover in this market suddenly dropped due to a firm from outside the county charging a much lower rate than ourselves and offering free collection and delivery every week. This firm specialised in re-forging and sharpening these tools, they had pneumatic equipment to press the chisels and points to shape therefore eliminating the laborious process of hammering each tool. Occasionally we still re-forge and sharpen the odd few for local builders and stone masons who do not possess an account with tool sharpening firms.

Our work now however had to embrace other more interesting techniques, a new direction was required; in what way could the enjoyable craft of forge-work provide us with a viable economic future?

I have long enjoyed the forging and creation of sculptural shapes inspired by natural forms. Garden sculpture plays another important role in the work we produce; it is a superb avenue to exercise ones imagination and creativity. Often when submitting work for exhibition I have to write a short statement regarding my work and I would like to think the following words say it all:

'Iron is an earthy element, smelted from its ore and wrought in the Smith's hearth in order to attain its final shape and form. At white heat it can be hammer-welded and possesses a fluidity almost characteristic of molten glass. These unique properties enable the material to express the depth of exploration and feeling latent within my work especially when married to other 'earthy' materials such as stone, glass, ceramics and polished agate.

Ideas, inspiration and images for my work are often sown as seeds which remain dormant in my mind for some considerable time before awaking fruition as a basis for sculptural form. The final result often bears little resemblance to the original image, only captivating brief memories and glimpses of texture and movement and colour.

For myself the foremost quality of expression in my work and the most essential ingredient can be summed up in one small word 'Flow'. A static object is brought to life when flowing form has been employed within its exploitation of aesthetics, dynamics and movement.'

This is an aspect of our craft that I enjoy above everything else, many folk would never imagine that hot iron and steel has such sculptural qualities and can be hammered and shaped into such beautiful forms. I have had numerous clients who having employed a designer to makeover their garden, then wished to commission a sculptural centre-piece, a focal point providing that extra something that their neighbours have not!

Gradually throughout many years of blacksmithing, I have assembled a portfolio of the numerous sculptures I have made. In fairness to our clients however, I will never repeat or copy a particular sculpture that has been previously commissioned, therefore making each item individual and unique, plus the added bonus of ensuring that one's next commission will present another creative challenge to attempt. Every sculptor however possesses his own unique style or signature and I care to assume that any one who is familiar with my work and when seeing a piece for the first time, will recognise that I have had a hand in the design, its making or both.

The conservation and restoration of antique ironwork requires an in-depth experience of specialist techniques and processes allied to the study of the history of period architecture and materials used. Such knowledge can only be acquired over many years of working on a numerous variety of projects, working with conservation officers, architects, historians, archaeologists and representatives from organisations responsible for such work such as English Heritage, the National Trust and Ecclesiastical institutions.

The main problem which occurs all too frequently is the lack of understanding of many clients and even architects, who simply believe that all professional metalworkers are capable of such work! Much of our decorative ironwork today is manufactured by metal fabricators who buy in ready made scrolls, twists, finials and components that have been cheaply mass produced in other countries. The railings, gates and screens are then mig-welded together, powder-coated and sold cheaply to decorate modern housing. The blacksmith who forges his scrolls with loving care, observing all correct terminations and technique now cannot possibly compete with the fabricator on price when producing ironwork for this type of market. I am however filled with anger when I frequently see ironwork destined for historical and period settings, listed buildings and conservation areas, which have been manufactured, assembled and installed by fabricators using the every day techniques which they apply to ordinary domestic ironwork. Would for example anyone accept an oak cabinet made with a fillet of glue round every joint? Therefore why should we accept the same in our craft? All ironwork produced before the advent of the electric welder has clean, crisp precise corners, scrolls, leaves and frames are joined together by traditional techniques including tenon joints, the use of collars, rivets and fire-welding.

Anyone wishing to study this aspect of our craft in order to practice restoration and conservation has to begin with a project which will not be above their capabilities, advice must clearly be sought from those having a legacy of experience in the craft. A clear programme, list and description of the necessary work for each project should be drawn up and checked with clients, architects, conservation officers etc before commencement of work.

One of the first restoration projects that came our way happened to be when a local conservator came to the forge bringing an Elizabethan chandelier, one of only two of its type known to exist; this beautiful piece of ironwork had come to grief in a huge fire that had nearly destroyed a famous country house. The fire had engulfed two thirds of the building and the chandelier which had been made in the design of a globe that supported a number of branched candle sconces had been damaged almost to the point of no repair. The central globe feature, consisting of a number of delicate iron scrolls, had been flattened when one of the main beams supporting the ceiling of the ballroom had fallen to the floor.

'Can anything be done?' asked the conservator. Not wishing to appear defeated, I replied 'Anything is possible!' However I made the mistake of hurriedly under estimating a price to which I became beholden and which I was to regret later on! 'There is a photograph of the chandelier in the Victoria and Albert Museum,' the conservator informed, 'I will endeavour to have a copy for you to look at.' Sure enough a few days later I received two clear photographs of the chandelier taken in its original situation.

Using an oxy-acetylene flame we carefully cleaned the ironwork with a bronze wire brush and opened the joining collars. The delicate scrolls seemed capable of restoration and the iron itself in spite of its age proved to be in excellent condition.

Gradually the many individual components were reformed to their original shape and finally after many hours of meticulous and painstaking work the assembled chandelier had been restored to its former glory. The project had taught us a great deal and although our original quote did not nearly pay us for the time we had spent upon the work, the experience had been necessary, educational and worthwhile. We had now to obtain more work of this nature and ensure we charged accordingly.

The following week, an architect contacted us asking if we could restore an ancient weathervane that had been taken down from the spire of a village church in Nottinghamshire. The cockerel, a three dimensional bird, hammered from copper sheet was basically in sound condition, and its verdigris coating having no detrimental effect. The two hundred year old ironwork and its decorative scrolls however, had suffered acute corrosion over the years and one of the copper letters of the cardinal points had long since broken away from the frame and had completely disappeared. The ironwork had to be taken apart, cleaned and the most seriously corroded components replaced using wrought iron as the material, therefore replacing like for like.

There is always confusion between the different meanings applied to the terms 'Restoration' and 'Conservation'. To conserve means to preserve the existing, whereas restoration allows for the piece to be restored to its former glory and be indistinguishable in appearance from its original condition. The question is, how much of the original is to be conserved and how much we have to replace? I generally take the point of view that if more than one third of the original is corroded to the point of non-existence, a complete identical replacement part in the same material is necessary, though each case scenario has to be judged on its own merits.

Occasionally other factors fall into the equation, mainly considerations appertaining to the future maintenance and prevention of corrosion. The welding of manganese bronze or stainless steel locating stubs to ironwork that is to be fixed into stone is sometimes insisted upon by architects and heritage monitoring institutions. Again each case scenario has to be judged upon its own merits.

Conservation work is interesting and challenging, it requires experience and specialist knowledge. It is a realm where there are always new aspects to be learned and is generally well paid.

On one particular occasion our local district Conservation Officer phoned to arrange an important meeting. He asked if we could assist him with a railing re-instatement project in the local country market town of Bellington, well known for its Georgian, Victorian and Edwardian architecture.

County Council and European funding, together with a sizeable Heritage Lottery Grant had been raised to pay for a revamp of many period buildings in the borough. The residents of one street in particular had been offered a sixty percent grant aid towards the cost of reproducing and re-instating the period iron gates and railings that once adorned the front of their dwellings before they were dismantled and removed for the war effort.

It was in May when I first heard about this project, which had to be completed by the end of the year otherwise the European funding would cease to be available. A firm of consultants had been given the task of discovering the design of the original railings and had been paid a sizable sum of money to produce an in-depth study and report. After months of so called research, their report ended with these immortal words, 'As far as we are aware there are no surviving records or photographs showing any of the ironwork in King Street before it had been removed during the war.' The survey contained many photographs of existing ironwork in other areas of the town, however alas nothing from King Street.

I asked the Conservation Officer if he would allow me to produce my own survey at a price, his reply being that if I came up with the results, he would pay the fee we negotiated. Immediately following our meeting I placed an advert in the Bellington Standard asking if anyone possessed any photographs of King Street taken before or after the war and offered £20 if they would allow me to take a photocopy of each one. Sure enough photographs materialized, many showing the original ironwork before it was removed, though a great deal of enhancement had to be achieved before I was able to ascertain the exact shape of the finials and motifs. A number of the houses had railings consisting of large cast iron decorative panels and cast iron gates that had been produced at a foundry now non-existent. The large cast iron stubs of these panels had been left leaded into the stone copings of the wall.

The conservation builder, Edward Blunt, had been chosen to rebuild and repair the walls, piers and copings in preparation for the ironwork to be placed in position. Edward remarked that his Grandmother had lived in number 72 King Street and that he still possessed an old photograph showing her standing outside her house in 1936. Edward loaned me this photograph which showed clearly the railings and gate in position. Fortunately, I knew of a house with these railings on a wall that required much repair together with the original gate. The owner agreed to loan us these panels in order for the foundry to use them as patterns, provided we rebuilt the wall and re-instated the railings.

Residents who wished to commission a railing re-instatement had to observe the protocol of planning permission, though they were assured this would certainly be granted. The procedure happened to be a costly process requiring an architect to prepare five copies of the necessary detailed drawings to scale: 1) of the ironwork, 2) the view of the property as now (existing), 3) the view as it would be with the ironwork in situ (proposed) 4) a plan to scale showing the situation in relation to the property and 5) a description of the proposed work.

The production of these drawings by an architect is a costly process and can take up a large slice of the grant aid and therefore I asked the Conservation Officer if I could prepare the drawings myself using a photo montage technique on the computer. My idea was to sketch the ironwork components, scan them into the computer, remove the white background, duplicate and arrange them to scale using a professional drawing package, finally superimposing the design of the railings on to the digital photograph showing exactly how the ironwork would appear realistically in situ. Although I made a charge for this work the cost was nowhere near an architect's fee, however the client had to agree to myself undertaking the work.

September arrived and the tedious beaurocratic process of grant applications and planning had finally run their course. A total of sixteen residents of King Street had decided to proceed with the reinstatement of railings and gates at the front of their properties and I only had four months to complete the work.

The Conservation Officer hastily called a site meeting with Edward in order to ascertain a 'modus operandi', a programme and schedule of the work that lay ahead. Edward seemed far from happy! 'At the moment my men are completing work on a large house at the other end of Town' he said. 'We are behind schedule and I can't see how I can spare them to prepare all the properties on King Street in readiness for you to commence this work!' 'The properties at 21 and 22 require their front walls taken down and the cheap nasty bricks scrapped.' ' The houses at 57 and 34 require their walls and copings dismantled and the materials stored ready for cleaning and re-building back as original.' 'The ash tree in the front garden of number 54 has to be uprooted and skipped, the front hedge at 34 must be removed and the concrete block copings in front of number 15 have to be taken up for disposal.' The two men left in order to attend to their agenda for the day with the Conservation Officer looking unhappy knowing his head would be on the bureaucratic chopping block if this project would not be completed on time.

I turned and glanced at John and he grinned, he knew exactly what I was thinking and I nodded in agreement. A skip was ordered and we began work, having taken out of the back of my pickup sledge hammers, spades, shovels, crowbars and a wheel barrow that we had brought along in anticipation of this work, though neither Edward or the Conservation Officer knew what we had planned. The skip was delivered within the hour and by that time we had already demolished the front walls of 21 and 22. The residents watched in eager anticipation and relief knowing that something was happening at last! As the day progressed, hedges and trees were uprooted, walls in a bad state of repair were taken down and the bricks stored in order to be rebuilt in the following weeks. The residents regularly made us cups of tea and coffee and even helped barrow the waste to the skip. John worked furiously without stopping for a rest, he happened to be an extremely strong young man, so much so that one of the residents asked him if he was ready for another can of spinach? At nine in the evening, all the work which Edward had described had been completed, John and I were now completely exhausted however we were pleased and elated with what we had achieved that day.

Edward and the Conservation Officer returned to King Street the following morning, they were completely flabbergasted upon seeing how the street had changed overnight. I had been somewhat apprehensive, wondering how Edward would take the surprise and if he would be angry that we had trespassed into his territory. This however happened not to be the case and therefore we were now able to proceed with the project.

The foundry had been informed of the project, their business was a small concern, a father and son team who specialised in one-off or small quantities of castings in aluminum, bronze and cast iron. They worked from an old wartime corrugated Nissan hut in an industrial estate in Nottinghamshire. The workshop itself would seem to have belonged to a grimy Victorian industrial area located somewhere in the Black Country, indeed the dark building covered from floor to ceiling in layers of black sand, grime and coke dust illuminated by the flames of the furnace presented a picture of an abject and abysmal working environment.

Acquiring the castings on time meant constant visits to the foundry, in fact this now became my biggest worry. However they soon realized that we were to be their main customer and bread and butter for the next few months. They eventually conformed to the routine of collection and supply that we required. The builders eventually appeared on site and began their work in earnest, the King Street railing re-instatement project was well under way.

At three o'clock on New Year's Eve, I carefully applied the last few touches of paint to the railings at number 57, being extremely close to completing the whole project. A few snowflakes began to fall and as the daylight faded, the house owner brought me out a cup of coffee spiced with a large tot of festive cheer. 'Very well done!' he said as I carefully replaced the lid on the pot of paint. I looked down the road and although the light was fading by the minute, I could still see the transformation that our ironwork had made to King Street and I couldn't help but shed a small tear as I packed up to go.

Chapter 11
Fires in new places

Having arrived back at the forge after the New Year's break, we had to concentrate on the many back orders that had accumulated whilst we were busy with the King Street railing re-instatements. Obviously we cannot turn small orders away; the customer ordering a small fire grate one day may tomorrow be commissioning a large pair of gates.

Indeed, it happened to be a fire grate that I was working on when the telephone rang; a call that resulted in a complete redirection of our business once again. The call came from Vera, the partner of Richard, the blacksmith at Lower Britwood. Vera informed me that Richard had decided to sell his equipment as he had decided to quit Blacksmithing, having been offered work as a welder at a local engineering company. John and I journeyed back to Lower Britwood and bought all the blacksmithing equipment including power hammer, forges, anvils, drilling machine, lathe, and a multitude of blacksmithing tools and as Richard no longer wished to rent the workshop, we re-applied to the Estate in order to retake the lease.

The Estate was only too willing to have us back and hence we terminated our lease at Moslingham Forge.

The relocation and setting up at Lower Britwood was fortunately financed by the profit we had made by the railing restoration work at Bellington, however it took far longer than expected. Roger, our next door neighbour at Moslingham helped immensely by transporting the heavy machinery and equipment. We were weeks setting up the workshop to meet my requirements and with an additional power-hammer, together with two other forge hearths, we were well on the way to the realisation of my dream; the setting up of a Blacksmithing School.

The move and subsequent work to the building was indeed proving more costly than I had first envisaged, we had to install a toilet, washroom, shower and outside a septic tank. There were repairs to the roof, converting a hayloft to an office, a cowshed to a demonstration room complete with two additional forge hearths and the acquisition of a site portacabin in order to provide computer and display facilities.

One morning in January, I arrived at the forge in order to begin work on a public art commission that myself and Helen had been commissioned for a local town park. The previous evening had been exceptionally cold and a consignment of steel bars delivered earlier that morning had frozen to the floor outside the building where the lorry driver had dropped them down from the side of the wagon. Perhaps later on in the morning when the suns rays had warmed the ground, it would be easier to bring the steel inside and place it on the rack. I made to walk round the edge of a steel bench when I tripped, falling and smashing my right arm on the edge of the one inch thick steel plate which covered the frame of the bench. The pain was horrific and when I attempted to stand, I realised my arm had been badly broken and happened to be flopping up and down as if only being held together loosely in a bag of flesh! John helped me sit down on the nearest available seat whilst he phoned for the ambulance, the wait seemed like an eternity, he made a small cup of strong tea in order to help me cope with the severe shock which had engulfed my system. I had turned extremely pale and dizzy and now my incoherent speech stuttered, 'How much longer?'

I desperately needed medication to ease the pain it seemed to be a foretaste of hell!

The ambulance arrived, one could hear the sirens as it journeyed along the narrow country lanes and after an initial brief diagnosis I was carried inside the vehicle and sped off to the County Hospital some ten miles distant. Helen by this time was approaching the forge. She saw the ambulance pass by and upon reaching the building met John stepping into his vehicle. John informed her of what had happened and the pair had a brief discussion of how best to help and deal with the situation that morning. John decided to go home and inform my wife that I had been taken to hospital and to arrange the clothes and toiletries that I would require as it seemed obvious that I would not be discharged that day. Helen quickly sped off to the hospital and joined me waiting to be seen by the doctor on duty at the Accident and Emergency department.

The A and E happened to be extremely busy that morning and therefore I resigned myself to a long and painful wait even though I had been given some powerful pain killers to ease my discomfort. As if we hadn't already been through enough trauma that morning, we were destined for even more to come! Suddenly, without any warning a prisoner accompanied by a young prison warder detached himself from his guard and swung a huge and violent blow upon a doctor innocently emerging from one of the rooms. Absolute pandemonium broke out as security staff bravely rushed forward to immobilise and contain the patient. Eventually when peace happened to be restored, I had to walk to the x-ray department and in a nearby corridor wait for a further length of time until they were ready to take a photograph of the inside mechanism of my right arm.

I spent four days in hospital during which further x-rays were taken, when the Consultant finally came to inform me of the prognosis, I heard the news that I was dreading, my right arm had been broken in eight places and that it would be an extremely long time before I would be capable of hammering again, that is, if I were ever to hammer again! It took a few minutes before the news eventually begun to sink in, my feelings were similar to the prisoner in the condemned cell shortly after judgement had been decreed. I seriously wondered if now was the time to pack everything in however I had others to consider and couldn't throw my work force on to the scrap heap along with my self! We still had much to achieve in the workshop and it seemed that my role would be a supervisory one. However, I had confidence that I could lead a team of excellent blacksmiths i.e. John, Helen and our apprentice Tim.

Two months passsed and even though my arm had not been taken out of plaster the consultant allowed me to drive, providing the moment I felt any difficulty in doing so I would report the situation to him. Being able to drive gradually gave me the confidence that I would not finally end my existence on the 'scrap heap' and I therefore began to plan out carefully how to steer the ship through turbulent waters.

I now had the opportunity to realize my dream of setting up a Blacksmithing School, teaching the craft and ensuring the traditional skills would be passed on to the next generation. Gradually we acquired more forge hearths and anvils. Initially I advertised courses locally beginning with evening classes and individual tuition and although being unable to hammer myself, I managed to talk our students through the processes they had to learn. It is said, 'If you see, you often don't remember, if you hear, then frequently you forget, but if you do, you always learn!'

I decided to have a website geared to advertising both our work and our courses. Knowing initially nothing about websites, I made the mistake of asking an amateur web enthusiast to construct one for me and totally regretted the decision. Firstly whenever I required changes to be made, I often had to wait an inordinate length of time for them to happen and as course dates, times and alterations require regular changes, I therefore required a professional site, content managed, with an administration section where I could change images and information when required.

The site I have now is in my opinion one of the foremost blacksmithing web-sites in the world, it is at the top of the front page of most search engines. It performs all my administration, even to notifying the accommodation providers of course bookings. The website also contains a three minute video advertising our courses and to date has proved its worth many times over.

Time slowly passed by without being able to use a hammer properly in fact I had no control over where the hammer would land upon the anvil. Although my muscles were still fairly strong, swinging a hammer seemed to be similar to swinging a weight on the end of a piece of string. My desire to be creative happened to be thwarted by the injury I had received and in order to retain my sanity, embarked upon a completely new project, one that occupied the majority of my time until I had fully recovered and was able to resume my normal work.

The railing re-instatement work that we had achieved for King Street had given me an idea; the plans we had submitted to the County Council had involved the production of a realistic photo montage showing exactly how the proposed ironwork would look in relation to its surroundings. Surely, I thought, this time-saving method of producing drawings and designs could be useful to many other Blacksmiths.

The seeds of 'Fired Imagination', my computer design package for blacksmiths', were sown and I began the enormous task of producing beautiful pencil drawings and shaded sketches of all the forged ironwork components I could possibly imagine. I scanned every drawing into the computer and working in a photographic programme, I removed the white in the picture leaving the drawing itself with a transparent background. By categorizing the images into sections such as Flat Bars, Wavy Bars, Curved Bars, Round Bars, Scrolls, Twists, Joints, Flowers, Leaves, Forged animal heads, Traditional gates, Contemporary gates, Finials etc. etc., I began to assemble a virtual collection of hundreds and hundreds of decorative components. These images could then be grouped together in order to compose complete drawings of architectural ironwork that could be superimposed upon photographs of the intended situation and therefore producing realistic, virtual images of the ironwork in situ.

The task of producing 'Fired Imagination' took eighteen months, even to the extent of printing a reference book giving thumbnail images and necessary information on how to use the package. I used a well known drawing programme in order to import, resize and manipulate the images and before I began to sell the package on my website I had numerous opportunities to test it out for real.

A couple came to the forge, wishing to commission a pair of gates for their large bungalow. Having discussed the available budget which they had set aside for the gates and discovering they wished the ironwork to be of a contemporary design, I made an appointment to visit their house in order to present them with a suitable design. After taking a digital photograph of the front gateway, I took my laptop inside and with the clients looking on, produced a design to their liking. My next step was to import the photograph of their driveway into the computer and superimpose the gate I had designed in between the brick entrance piers.

The clients gazed in awe at the resultant image that seemed so realistic one would have assumed the gates were actually there!

I have since sold copies of the CD to blacksmiths in many countries. The great factor being that the library of images can be added to as and when new images are required, providing one has the ability to draw and sketch to a reasonable standard. 'Fired Imagination' is much easier to use than many of the 'Cad' programmes that engineers and architects employ, the package produces drawings which have the character of traditional draughtsmanship, allowing artistic light and shade to add realism and character to the presentation. 'Fired Imagination' can also be used to produce quickly the drawings required for planning permission, the services of which can command a design fee, therefore being extremely helpful when offsetting ones expenses in a large project. I am now in the process of working on 'Fired Imagination' version 2, containing many more component images, this time in 'Photoshop' format complete with a PDF catalogue of thumbnail drawings for quick and easy reference.

Gradually we continued making improvements to our teaching facilities, with additional forges and anvils. Our 'Basic Beginners' course required (and incidentally still does) students to make a beautiful hanging basket bracket containing techniques almost reaching intermediate standard. I spent four months producing annotated drawings of every stage in the manufacture of this bracket, which have been laminated and pinned to the wall of the Demo room in order to provide a visual reference. The cost of our three day courses were designed to include meals at a local restaurant but not accommodation. Local B &B s have greatly benefited from the trade we have given them.

We have run many intermediate courses at the forge including: Forged metal sculpture, Bladesmithing and Pattern-welding, The conservation and restoration of period and historical ironwork and Toolmaking for Blacksmiths, therefore establishing ourselves as one of the leading centres providing private Blacksmithing tuition in the country.

Ten months had now elapsed since breaking my arm and though seven of them had now healed, one large break had thwarted Nature's ability to mend without the assistance of surgery and pinning. On one occasion I duly attended my regular three monthly appointment with the consultant when he asked me if I would like the good news or the bad? My stomach began to tremble, 'Whatever now?' I thought. 'What's the good news then?' I asked apprehensively. 'We can finally operate to repair the last break,' he said, ' however the bad news is that the break is extremely close to a nerve, that if severed and will cause you to lose some of the movement in your right hand!' 'What is the percentage risk?' I asked, 'Five percent' came the reply. 'Then we'll go for it!' I exclaimed. Three weeks later a letter arrived offering a place at Busford County Hospital and after a further four weeks I had been admitted to the aptly named Moslingham Ward, a slightly humorous and poignant reminder of a previous chapter of my life.

After initial x-rays and tests the consultant gave the final go-ahead for the operation the following afternoon. The anaesthetist gave me the first of two injections, which would render me oblivious to the delicate surgery that would be applied to my arm; there was now no going back. I lay on the trolley completely surrendered to their knowledge, competence and surgical expertise.

The time happened to be one o'clock in the morning when I first began to regain consciousness; at first, I had difficulty in realising where I happened to be. The surgeon had strapped the new plaster to my chest in order to immobilize my arm and prevent damage to the work he had done. As I gradually came round however, I became aware of an excruciating pain in my arm. I called for the nurse who informed me of a plunger I could press that would inject morphine into my vein, therefore helping to ease the suffering and discomfort. Unfortunately and unnoticed, the plastic tube became detached from the pump and without realising it, all I achieved was to pump the fluid on to the sheets of the bed. My first night after the operation had not been made easy by the detachment of the pump, in fact I spent the first few hours after the operation in sheer agony and when daylight eventually came, the nurse discovered what had happened and gave me pain relief in tablet form which eventually took effect.

Four days after the operation, the consultant gave me permission to leave the hospital, with an appointment to see him in four weeks time. He gave me strict instructions to rest and above all to stay away from work. Once again I had to direct operations at the forge from home; my mobile phone bill would certainly be far more expensive than usual. The four weeks seemed like an eternity, however somehow my arm felt pleasantly different, even though being encapsulated in a full cast of plaster.

A morning spent waiting to undergo a further series of x-rays preceded my meeting with the consultant, Mr Keightly, who carefully studied the photographs before informing me that he was extremely pleased with the progress so far. He instructed me to keep the plaster on for three more weeks, after which and following a further appointment and continued improvement, I would be able to have the plaster removed. I returned home hopeful and with the realization that Rome wasn't built in a day. I still had to be patient and extremely careful if I were ever to hammer again!

I will never forget the day when they removed the cast that had contained my arm. I had had very little sleep the previous night, lying awake wondering if my arm would have seized and be totally incapable of movement. As the nurse carefully cut through the plaster, I just hoped and prayed that once liberated my injured limb would eventually be restored to its original capability and condition. This, however was not to be, what little available movement there was happened to be painful and stiff. The nurse then placed my arm in a sling, telling me to exercise and free my arm gradually in order to acquire increased mobility naturally and in a comfortable manner.

Constantly and gradually exercising the arm began to bear fruit, after one week I dispensed with the sling and after fourteen days I could lift a small hammer and move it up and down. This I continued to do until I could hammer a small piece of hot iron gently upon the anvil. My next appointment with the consultant had been made for eight weeks after the plaster had been removed. On that day I first had to have an x-ray before being seen by the consultant. This time I felt confident, some how I knew success had been achieved.

I still became slightly nervous however as I sat in the queue outside the consultants room, eventually my turn arrived and having entered, sat apprehensively as the consultant studied my x-rays. I could see clearly where the break had been and also the titanium plate holding the once broken bone by means of an extremely neat row of screws, which left me thinking that I would be worth more as scrap when I eventually die. The consultant examined my arm and asked me if I could touch first my head and then my back, he asked me if I could lift anything and I proceeded to hold a chair above my head. He finally asked me to push against his hand and immediately said to ease off. 'Do I need any physiotherapy?' I asked, 'Not at all' he replied, 'I'm certain you've achieved enough already.'

Often folk ask me how I managed to regain the strength back into my arm after the accident and my reply is this:

'I took the advice of an old blacksmith who related how he acquired his strength as a young apprentice. He held a 5 lb potato bag out and practiced moving his arm up and down, up and down. Next he graduated to a 10 lb potato bag and to a 25lb bag, moving his arm up and down up and down! Eventually he moved on to a 50lb bag repeating the same exercise and finally a 100lb potato bag, up and down, up and down! Then he began to fill them with potatoes !!!'

Potatoes

Chapter 12
Raking out the Ashes

Sundays were normally our day of relaxation and enjoyment, Ann enjoyed travelling to the seaside; she found hill walking an anathema, whereas a journey to the coast and walks along the seafront and beach were nothing less than a heavenly experience of sheer enjoyment and delight.

Frequently, we combined our excursion to the seaside by paying a visit to my adoptive Father who had retired to the coast some years before, shortly after this move his wife, my adoptive mother had died after suffering from cancer that had been diagnosed some months earlier. Often we took Dad to enjoy Sunday lunch at a local hostelry before retiring for afternoon tea and conversation at his bungalow on a local estate.

Since the tragic death of his wife, Father had led an active life both as a churchgoer, local preacher, and public speaker. He gave illuminating and interesting talks on the life of the Bronte family of Howarth in Yorkshire. Victorian and Edwardian classics were his enjoyment and passion. Father happened to be a person of great intelligence and integrity, an extremely popular person, well known for his charitable work in the community.

On one particular occasion, as we returned from an excellent Sunday lunch at a country pub in order to relax in conversation and reminiscence, Father appeared from his bedroom and handed me two aged envelopes, each containing a faded browning letter, obviously written many years previous. 'I can't ever remember you enquiring about your roots', he exclaimed. 'I have here correspondence from your real mother a short time after she handed you over to us for adoption. I have no idea if she is still alive, however you can have the letters for your own keeping, though I believe it's now possibly too late for you to discover what happened to her, that's if you really have the desire to.' I gazed at the manuscripts with interest; the neat and legible handwriting seemed somehow to be the work of an extremely intelligent and caring person. The ink in places seemed slightly smudged as if a couple of tear drops had fallen upon the letters at some moment of composition.

The earlier of the two had been written a few days after my adoption; Dorothy had obviously been a nurse during the war and had subsequently worked for a short period at the Great Ormond Street Hospital. The letter expressed her best wishes for the child and related how she would soon be leaving her employment to begin a new life in distant places. She had served her country as a nurse, attending our wounded soldiers at a hill station in Burma throughout the war and travelling many miles happened now to be part and parcel of her life. Some weeks later my mother, named Dorothy, posted a second letter to my adoptive parents describing how she had terminated her nursing career in order to enjoy a brief respite in Devon before setting out to live a new life in another country. Her letter stated that this would be her final correspondence to my adoptive parents, she would soon be moving to distant places and future contact would cease. She wished them and the child God bless and would depart confident that I would have a good Christian upbringing.

Upon leaving my Father that Sunday evening, I became increasingly agitated and apprehensive, wondering how I could possibly learn more about my origins and roots. I had little sleep that night and for some unknown reason I had an acute desire to discover what had happened, who had been responsible and why had I been handed over to a third party? Psychologically I had been uprooted; I felt unsettled, somewhere out there lay the answer, would I ever find out the truth?

Monday dawned, tired through lack of sleep I arrived at work, my mind in turmoil. At three o'clock in the afternoon I could stand it no longer, I picked up the phone and dialled directory enquiries. The home address of the last letter that we had received from my Mother had been 17 Hill Court, Snarsbury, Devon. It seemed however that I had drawn a blank, no one of my original name of Pope happened to be residing at that address.

It had occurred to me that Mother may have been on holiday at a guest house in Devon, though it had seemed more probable she would have been staying with either friends or relations. I realised I could be clutching at straws, however I just felt that I had to make a move. My second call was made to the electoral role office in Exeter, where I enquired if anyone by that name had been residing at that address at the time I had been born. Again I drew a blank being informed that their records did not go back that far. 'Could you tell me who is residing there now?' I asked. The voice at the other end replied that Regulations prevented him from divulging such information. 'But I'm trying to find my Mother,' I exclaimed, 'All right', the man answered, 'I will tell you his name, however I will not give you his telephone number, you will have to find that out for yourself.'

Fortunately the directory enquiries supplied this information and the person answered the telephone, however only to say he knew of no one by the name of Pope in the vicinity.' 'There is however,' he stated, 'an old lady living at number one, she happened to be born in the dwelling and has lived there all her life. She would know if anyone by that name ever lived at number17 and although now in her eighties, the lady is extremely coherent. Hang on I will find her phone number.'

Nervously I dialled the lady in question, the time now being half past three. 'I knew Dot!' she exclaimed, 'I happened to go to school with her, she went abroad immediately after the war and as far as I know she has never returned. Her half sister however lives at number 10, I believe that Dot is still alive.' A shiver ran down my spine, perhaps I happened to be on track at last, I rang her half sister and related my story.'I never knew Dot had a child.' said her half sister Joan. 'Dot journeyed to South Africa after the war and has never returned, she married in 1960 and her husband passed away in 1972.''Dot worked as a nurse in Johannesburg and is now retired, however she is shortly returning to pay us an extended visit, it may even be that she stays here for the rest of her life.' 'When is she coming over?' I asked. 'Next Wednesday' came the reply and I stood shaking in my boots. 'Is she staying with yourself?' I trembled. 'Dot is staying for a couple of weeks with my son, her nephew, at Sidcup in Kent. Jim is a sergeant in the Met Police, I'll give you his number.'

Obviously through being in the police, Jim became extremely suspicious upon receiving my call. He asked if he could visit us the following day and requested he be able to read the two letters that Dot had written in 1946. I therefore agreed and after replacing the handset, walked away feeling in need of something slightly stronger than mere coffee. I phoned my wife and yelled, 'I'VE FOUND HER! I'VE FOUND HER!' The time now happened to be four fifteen, events had unfolded fast, perhaps too quickly, it had been a shock to the system and almost uncanny. The coincidences of all this happening seemed less plausible than winning the National Lottery. I had spent half of my life not knowing anything regarding my real mother. I had been handed two letters the previous day that had been written by her shortly after the war. Within the space of one hour and fifteen minutes I had discovered that, still alive and well, Dot happened to be returning to this country the following week for the first time since she had left the country shortly after the war. Unknown to myself however, more of the strangest happenings were to follow!

Ann and I met Jim and his wife, Sue, the following day outside the Castle Hotel in the city centre. We took them to the restaurant inside for lunch, during which we unfolded our story to date. Jim agreed that the handwriting in the letters was that of Dot and produced a photograph of my mother in her army uniform taken towards the end of the war. The picture showed a tall beautiful and charismatic, lady though I suspected that in old age she would present a different picture. I happened to be pleased however that I had been privileged to have been born from such a seemingly wonderful lady.

Jim informed us that Dot had become a rather frail eighty year old who would probably be extremely tired after the long flight from Johannesburg to Heathrow. He suggested we allow a few days respite and time for her to recuperate after the journey before making contact and that we phone her at the weekend. 'Jim!' I exclaimed, 'we are staying ten miles from you on Saturday. Ten weeks ago, we booked our touring caravan into a local

Caravan Club site as we are demonstrating at a craft show in your area!' The latest sequence of events defied belief, I gazed towards the heavens wondering who had a hand in the unfolding drama to date?

That Friday, the 'Travelling Blacksmith's show' hit the road. Our vehicle towing the caravan had been fully loaded with portable forge, tools, stall, and ironwork for sale. I had difficulty in concentrating on my driving to the event; my mind was confused and focused only upon meeting my mother for the first time. My thoughts were in turmoil; problems presented themselves with increasing frequency, it did not seem that the meeting would be an easy affair. Perhaps she would not wish to face me after all these years and would she feel guilty in some way that handing her son over for adoption could be deemed the relinquishing of maternal responsibility, an abandonment of obligation and duty?

For my part, I became concerned as to whether I would feel any natural bonding towards her; how would my education, character and personality had differed from my present disposition if I had remained with her from birth? Would any obvious physical resemblance be immediately apparent and if so would my appearance be a poignant reminder of my natural Father, a person who yet I knew nothing about and perhaps such similarities would be disagreeable to her, bringing back memories of a past fraught with unhappiness and tension! I could not help fearing however that our meeting would turn out to be a completely unproductive and negative exercise, resulting in psychological trauma for both parties. Perhaps I should have sought counselling instead of rushing headlong into uncertainty!

Having arrived at the craft show, sited our caravan and set up our stand, I drove in search of a fish and chip shop to purchase our supper. Thoroughly tired, we finally laid our heads to sleep, though the nagging uncertainty of the morrow's promise left me tossing and turning in beads of perspiration.

I have seldom felt so long a day as our first days trading, nervously I glanced frequently at my watch. Somehow I could not seem to concentrate on my demonstrations, the audience unusually seemed completely disinterested. I simply could not perform as normal, a situation being reflected in our lack of sales for the day. We drove back to our caravan site at the end of the show, showered and changed in preparation of the arranged meeting. At six pm, as promised, I dialled Jim's phone, waiting with bated breath and apprehension. Jim answered the phone and immediately said 'Your Mother is waiting to meet you, the unfinished business she mentioned in her last letter happened to be the discovering of yourself. Do pay us a visit this evening and introduce yourself.'

As we approached Jim's house my heart beat rapidly, my pulse a racing rhythm of anticipation. We drove up and down the road for some time, seeking a space at the side where we could park. Eventually I observed in my rear mirror a small car driving away. I reversed down the road for approximately two hundred yards and after a seemingly long performance of forward and reverse, I managed to tuck our pickup truck into that small available space. Indeed the operation had been as if we had managed to fit a quart into a pint pot! In a state of great anxiety, I walked up the driveway and nervously knocked on the door. Moments later Jim greeted Ann and I, 'Come on in' were his words as he ushered us into the hall.

'At the end of the corridor stood a small grey haired old lady; she smiled and held out her hand. Feeling slightly embarrassed and perplexed, I considered whether I should shake the hand or show loving affection and hug her in the pretence that everything that had happened previously had finally been resolved. Standing in front of her and trembling nervously, I simply stuttered, 'How are you?' Mother stepped forwards in order to embrace her son and for one brief moment it seemed as if time had suddenly stopped. Jim turned to Ann and quietly suggested they left us alone for a while, giving us a short time to make our acquaintance.

Dot had eagerly been waiting and praying for this event to take place, a totally bizarre reunion of momentous occurrence. The meeting seemed as if for her part prayers had been well and truly answered; for my part however, many more questions had to be resolved before any future relationship could be envisaged. I had at last met my natural mother and this to me was only half the story. Mother for reasons unknown to myself seemed extremely determined that details of the other party to my conception would never be disclosed. For myself, the evening seemed to pass slowly. I couldn't help but detect a sense of uneasiness which prevailed throughout. Well thought out and polite conversation became a substitute for what should have been a joyous disclosure.

Jim agreed to bring Dot to our show the following day, where she could see for herself how we made our living and I hoped the event would provide a less formal venue proving the opportunity to break down barriers imposed by uncertainty and inhibition. Upon returning to our caravan I endeavoured to catch up on my previous sleepless nights, however I couldn't help but wonder if the meeting had begun to uncover a can of worms. Once again my brain became a hive of activity and conjecture; in retrospect, ought I to have let sleeping dogs lie?

The craft fair at which we were taking part also provided entertainment for its visitors by staging medieval re-enactment, folk-singers, Morris dancers and traditional street theatre. For this event we had purchased a brand new marquee some eight feet by twelve, consisting of a box frame construction covered by a blue and white striped tarpaulin. A lean-to at one end provided cover for myself whilst working upon the anvil with my portable forge blazing away to one side. We had indeed a smart professional set up, a travelling showcase for the ironwork that we had for sale and I felt proud that upon the first occasion it had been used, I could show it to my Mother, who I had met for the first time that previous evening.

Fine weather and brilliant sunshine had been forecast throughout the day and it felt as if a huge weight had been lifted from my shoulder. I felt optimistic that the show would be a memorable and enjoyable experience for my mother; at least I would be meeting her on my own territory, being able to perform and impress her with the entertainment I could provide.

At two pm as I began to manufacture another of my ram's head pokers, I noticed Jim, his wife and my mother standing to one side of the small crowd of onlookers who had gathered to watch my demonstration. I acknowledged Mother with a brief wave as I continued forging the red hot steel, describing the processes involved to a fascinated audience. The demonstration became a great feat of entertainment and it seemed as if I were performing to the Queen herself. Immediately I held up the finished item for spectators to admire, I won an accolade of applause and my act was quickly followed by a small group of folk singers, who began to entertain everyone in front of my stand. They invited me to join in as I often did, being an enthusiastic singer and blessed with a powerful tenor voice. The musical performance, in full harmony, had an electric effect upon the audience, our song being the powerful 'Spencer the Rover' written by the well known folk song writer Bob Copper. Mother gazed in admiration, this happened to be her first real taste of England and after an absence of many years had proved to be a truly wonderful occasion.

Leaving my wife to look after our stall, I escorted my guests around the show ground. Mother seemed to relish every moment of the experience. Our visitors thoroughly enjoyed the occasion and thoroughly enthused, the ice began to break, we chatted amiably, a warmth of friendship developed and I looked forward to getting to know more about her. Returning to our stand I, spoke to a couple who had paged through my portfolio. They had waited patiently to enquire if we would be able to repair a broken length of cast iron railings at the side of the front garden of their house. The house, situated in Aldershot and being in a conservation area, required precise restoration of cast iron work broken after impact damage from a vehicle collision. We agreed to the repairs knowing that Mother had arranged to stay with her brother Fred in nearby Southampton. Mother invited us to stay at Fred's house and to meet other relations with whom I had never made acquaintance.

Two weeks later, John and I travelled to Aldershot in order to repair the railings in question. We had booked into a local B&B, envisaging the work to take no longer than one afternoon. Prior to our visit our clients had sent us photographs of the railing damage which had been caused by a vehicle collision some months earlier. We had brought with us a virtual mobile workshop that we set up outside the front garden of the house.

The damage had been localised to about one and a half meters of the railings, in all twenty seven breaks had to be welded using specialist welding rods consisting of pure nickel covered with a chemical coating in order to prevent oxidation and contamination of the weld. We had previously undertaken many similar commissions however, the situation here happened to be unusual in that the repairs in question happened to be within the centre of a large holly bush in an extremely dry and flammable condition.

Clambering into the centre of the holly bush, I realised how dangerous the task happened to be. John stood to one side armed with both Co2 and dry powder extinguishers as I addressed the risky task ahead. Several of the breaks were welded without any problems until John yelled that the tinder dry holly bush had caught alight, it quickly became one huge firework, which I happened to be in the centre of. An elderly couple walking by heard dire exclamations ensuing from the conflagration, they were reminded of religious education in their youth having been taught the story of Moses and the voice ensuing from the burning bush. Needless to say the couple fled the scene hoping they would escape the anger of the Lord. John realising my predicament immediately threw a bucket full of water over me and I escaped, thoroughly soaked, un-singed and still in one piece.

Holly Smoke

Chapter 13
Charred Memories

Having completed our work at Aldershot, John and I journeyed to Southampton to meet up again with my Mother, intending to stay for a few days and discover more of a family that until now I had never known. The time had turned five minutes past six and the late afternoon sunshine brightened the coastal road as we drove into the town. A myriad chorus of seagulls called, heralding our arrival. The rows of neat terraced houses, that had survived the war time blitz, stood out like gems among the dull concrete blocks of flats which had been built in the fifties to re-house those whose homes had been destroyed by the bombing.

Mother had now moved from Jim's house in Kent in order to meet up and stay with her younger brother Fred, a retired postman in his early seventies. Fred lived in a small, attractive, bay windowed terraced house painted light cream on the outside, one of a complete row overlooking the lower part of the town and harbour. He had a happy disposition and though small in stature he looked extraordinarily fit for his age. Being pleased to see us Fred welcomed John and I as long lost members of the family. His wife, Jenny, had prepared us all a meal of roast lamb, new potatoes and freshly cooked vegetables and afterwards over a glass or two of wine we enjoyed a conversation of discovery; yes, we had so much to find out about each other!

Fred had been an evacuee during the war and had stayed with a family a few miles from where I had been brought up. He remembered clearly my town, Nottingham and the village which had become his temporary home. My Mother reminisced her training as a nurse at the beginning of the war, however a few years earlier as a small girl, her mother, father and brother moved to Canada. She related how one day her father went out to seek work further afield, how she said good bye at the station and how he never returned. A year elapsed before her mother and children managed to scrape enough money together and return on a boat bound for England where they were cared for by her mother's relations in Devon.

Exercising extreme tact and diplomacy, I endeavoured to steer the conversation towards finding out about my real father. However, Mother appeared to detect the purpose of my questions and immediately changed the subject. She obviously had no intentions of unlocking any of her well kept secrets; if ever I were to discover the truth it certainly would not be soon.

Mother certainly had all her faculties about her, she came over as an extremely intelligent and mentally alert lady and although small, wrinkled and aged in appearance, had the ability to command the conversation, asserting her views with authority. Her life in South Africa had been secure and settled, apart from when her husband died. Dot however continued to practice as a nurse until she retired at the age of sixty two, her social life being supported by the white community and her Church, which happened to be an integral part of her life.

Dot asked how my parents were. She was pleased to learn that my adoptive father had been keeping well and also seemed extremely interested for some reason in my initial desire to become a blacksmith. The evening passed in a relaxed manner until Dot disclosed some information regarding her family, which for a moment had me freeze to the chair in which I was seated. Her grandfather had been the blacksmith at a well known village in the New Forest. As a young girl she had been to visit him many times and gave an accurate description of his forge and its situation alongside the only pub in the district.

I had never been to the New Forest and therefore suggested that next day we had an excursion to visit this place, to find out whether or not the forge or the building still existed. Dot agreed to this, especially as we had promised her lunch at the pub or a nearby hostelry. Once again I had difficulty in sleeping however this seemed to answer the question as to how or where I acquired my ability to hot forge steel. Perhaps it lay in my genes!

The following morning at breakfast, as I slowly munched a piece of toast, I enquired if Dot had spent much time in her grandfather's forge? 'I normally visited the place nearly every weekend,' she replied, 'I remember him shoeing horses and also repairing tools and machinery. In fact I remember some of his implements on display in the pub next door.'

We set out after breakfast and headed towards the New Forest; the landscape, being bathed in glorious sunshine with hardly a cloud in the sky and the famous wild ponies, presented an amazing sight, for although having owners, they are free to roam of their own accord for miles around.

Following a beautiful exploratory sight-seeing tour of the area, we arrived at our destination at twelve noon. As Dot had described, the village had only one pub, which probably would have been a Coaching Inn in the days of the horse drawn carriage. The village mainly consisted of stone cottages and many of the shops made their living selling gifts and souvenirs to the tourists and visitors exploring the area. A long, low, single storey building directly across the yard of the inn could have once been a forge and stables. It had the familiar pair of wooden doors across what probably had been the entrance to the Shoeing Shed. The building had been converted to a craft shop and gallery, though missing a chimney, which would have been certain proof that it once existed as a forge.

Although the craft shop had closed at that time for lunch it would, according to the notice on the door, re-open at two thirty pm. and therefore we decided to partake of a meal at the Inn itself and to visit the craft shop when it re-opened. Unfortunately, we could find no evidence of blacksmiths' artefacts and work in the pub itself. I therefore asked the landlord if he could impart any information relating to the inn having a working forge. He stated that having only recently bought the property, he had heard nothing regarding a forge ever being attached to the pub.

The Three Horseshoes Inn certainly had an apt name if it had once had a forge attached. The building had been altered in the late twenties, probably with a view to providing accommodation and extra rooms. As we ate our lunch, I enquired how many times my mother had travelled to visit her grandfather and as to where she stayed. Dorothy related how her mother (who had now lost her husband) journeyed by train to Southampton at least four times a year. Her grandfather arranged a pony and trap to collect and bring them to his house, where they stayed for a week at any one time.

Having replenished ourselves, we ventured in the direction of the long, low building situated to one side of the car park; the double doors were now open, its owner having now returned from lunch. In many respects the building reminded me of the local forge way back in my youth, the aged pantiled roof, its windows resembling those through which fascinated and spell bound I peered, watching the blacksmith at work.

The interior of the craft shop had now been thoroughly cleaned and the walls made cheerful with white emulsion, however I immediately spotted the first tell tale sign that the building had once been a forge. Above the large entrance door and held by a deep iron staple securely embedded into the massive solid oak lintel, proved to be an iron ring some three inches in diameter, almost identical to the one at my first forge at Cupwood. A ring that would help immobilise an unruly horse by tethering a hind leg, its hoof being elevated from the floor. These were however the only visible similarities between the local forge of my youth, the shelves, tables and beams within the interior were clinical in their appearance, not covered with layers of dust and grime.

Hand-made pottery, woodcarvings and jewellery, home-made toffee, greeting cards and hundreds of saleable souvenirs were displayed aesthetically within the building. The proprietor, a short but stocky middle aged man, seemed to be hovering a few feet away, diligently dusting pottery mugs arranged along the newly painted window sill, however quietly keeping guard on the many exhibits from possibly potential light fingered souvenir hunters.

Once inside, I introduced us to the owner and asked whether or not the building had once been a blacksmith's forge? 'I haven't been here very long,' the proprietor replied 'and we have certainly had a tremendous amount of work cleaning out these buildings and preparing our display.' ' However, the other week, I knocked down an internal wall only to reveal the original forge hearth and we have now made a feature of it. Come over here and have a look!'

I walked swiftly between two rows of glass show cases and on turning a corner came face to face with a brick hearth and canopy. I instantly recognised it as being an old blacksmith's forge, the small hand-made bricks surrounding where the tue iron had been were blackened by years of the heat of countless forge fires.

Suddenly I became overcome with awe and emotion as I gazed upon the hearth where my great grandfather had forged his living. 'I am hoping to acquire an old pair of bellows and an anvil in order to create a feature of the hearth,' explained the proprietor, 'the display would make an unusual attraction.' I seemed to find it impossible to take my eyes from gazing at what now seemed to have become a shrine to my great grandfather. Did his spirit somehow be gazing at us? Who or what had engineered this to happen? I turned to the proprietor and asked him when it was that he knocked down the wall to reveal the forge? He gave me the date and I froze! It happened to be the day my Mother came into the country!

Back to the beginning

Postscript

Dot remained in the UK, having eventually decided she would not return to South Africa. Jim undertook the complicated procedure of winding up Dot's affairs in Johannesburg from his home in Kent and the transfer of her goods and belongings to Devon, where she had decided to remain for the rest of her life. Jim had found a small council flat in the village of Sudford, twenty miles east of Exeter. Dot had been born in that village and it seemed only fitting that she should spend the rest of her days close to many of her relations in the area, who she knew in her early childhood, before the family moved elsewhere.

Dot became a member of the local church and regularly attended the services there. The ancient Norman church, situated on the summit of one of the highest hills nearby, could be seen for miles around. From the churchyard on a clear day one could discern the distant coast and the moor land plateau of Exmoor to the east. Having once been a nurse and served the country during the war, Dot was entitled to a small pension that could be backdated over a long period of time. The money due, together with other annuities, provided Dot with the means to receive a modest but comfortable existence at her flat.

The combination of running a business and living so far a way, prevented us from visiting my mother as often as I would have liked. In retrospect, I now wish I had made the effort more often to journey the many miles to her home in Devon, considering the short space of time we were blessed with her presence. We regularly conversed over the phone and on one particular occasion decided to combine a short visit and holiday at the same time.

Perhaps this time I would learn more about my roots, direct questions always seemed to face an insurmountable barrier of polite however obstinate evasiveness!

Leaving home in the early hours of the morning, my mind was once again focussed upon my ancestry, perhaps this time I would discover the whole truth, secrets which had been locked away for years within the confined depth of my mother's heart. The drive to Devon presented no problems, we encountered no hold ups, diversions or traffic jams and having only made one brief refreshment break, I considered that we had eventually arrived in record time.

Dot welcomed our arrival with open arms. She had prepared a hearty meal and afterwards, as we relaxed in front of the open fire, I endeavoured to manipulate and focus the conversation in order to resolve my ultimate question.

Eventually I leaned over and said, 'Dot, it has been wonderful discovering you as my real Mother and I know from what Jim had informed me that it had been your single wish to discover how your son had progressed since the day you entrusted me to my adoptive parents all those years ago.' 'Please forgive me however, I too have one more wish, that being to discover as to whom had been my real Father?' 'I now know from which side of the family I have acquired my ability as a blacksmith, however there are other aspects of me which have come from elsewhere and I would dearly wish to discover the truth.'

Mother sat back in her chair and stared into space, after a few silent moments, without looking me in the face, she replied, 'At the moment the time isn't right, perhaps one day!' I couldn't help notice however the tear which ran down the cheek of her wrinkled face and therefore decided I had no alternative but to postpone this subject of conversation to a more appropriate occasion.

A Gate

Our respite in Devon soon came to an end, we had taken Dot to visit many more of her relations in the South East and realised that she happened to be part of an enormous family. On the whole, I was cordially received, though I suspect a few regarded me as an object of curiosity in a rather stand offish manner.

Fond farewells are much fonder if both parties leave in an atmosphere of friendship and honesty. Somehow, I could not feel that Mother had been truly up- front and honest with my request in discovering who had been my father. I departed feeling sad and let down; I hardly said a word on the journey home. My quest had so far ended in failure!

One November evening, some eighteen months after we had first met my mother that evening in Kent, I received a phone call from Jim, informing us that Dot had suffered a severe heart attack and had been rushed into Hospital. Two hours later we received the sad news that she had passed away without regaining consciousness. Dorothy had finally ended her days in the village where she had been born; she had lived to a good old age of eighty six. Her ambition to return to England and be reunited with her son had been realised, her prayers had been answered. Ann and I hurriedly made preparations to journey down to Devon and attend the funeral at the local church. With tears in my eyes, I silently watched as they lowered her coffin into the freshly dug grave within the Churchyard, high up, overlooking the surrounding hills. Dot had found her peace, whereas I had to walk away knowing that my own questions would now probably never ever be resolved.

Ann and I have returned to Sudford since the date of Mother's funeral and each time placed a bouquet of flowers at her grave. I once donated a large Pascal candle holder to the church, a piece of work which I had designed and made specially at the forge back home, The church subsequently organised a special service in Dot's memory to dedicate the gift.

I have since learned to accept her wish to withhold the identity of my true father, knowing how kind and affectionate she had been in her life. After much heartache and thought, I have now come to forgive and respect her wishes, remembering Dot as one who had spent her life helping others in times of need and distress.

Floral Sculpture

Traditional Gates

Inglenook Fireplace

Entrance to a fairyland garden

Iron in the Blood

Iron in the Blood

Iron in the Blood